E 184 .I6 I617 2005

The Irish

DATE DUE

D1020285

THE IRISH

Other books in the
Coming to America series:

COMING TO AMERICA

THE IRISH

Karen Price Hossell, *Book Editor*

Bruce Glassman, *Vice President*
Bonnie Szumski, *Publisher*
Helen Cothran, *Managing Editor*
Laura K. Egendorf, *Series Editor*

GREENHAVEN PRESS
An imprint of Thomson Gale, a part of The Thomson Corporation

THOMSON

GALE

Detroit • New York • San Francisco • San Diego • New Haven, Conn.
Waterville, Maine • London • Munich

© 2005 Thomson Gale, a part of The Thomson Corporation.

Thomson and Star Logo are trademarks and Gale and Greenhaven Press are registered trademarks used herein under license.

For more information, contact
Greenhaven Press
27500 Drake Rd.
Farmington Hills, MI 48331-3535
Or you can visit our Internet site at http://www.gale.com

Cover credit: © Bettmann/CORBIS
Library of Congress, 39, 122, 169

LIBRARY OF CONGRESS CATALOGING-IN-PUBLICATION DATA
The Irish / Karen Price Hossell, book editor.
    p. cm. — (Coming to America)
Includes bibliographical references and index.
ISBN 0-7377-2154-5 (lib. bdg. : alk. paper)
    1. Irish Americans—History. 2. Immigrants—United States—History. I. Hossell, Karen Price, 1957– . II. Coming to America (San Diego, Calif.)
E184.I6I617 2005
973'.049162—dc22
                                        2004047582

Printed in the United States of America

CONTENTS

Chapter 1: Leaving Ireland

contributed to the ill health and deaths of many passengers.

Chapter 2: Life in the United States for Famine Immigrants

Chapter 3: Pain, Progress, and Assimilation

tected from identification and deportation. However, the terrorist attacks of September 11, 2001, have led to great scrutiny of all illegal immigrants.

Chapter 4: Portraits of Irish Americans

FOREWORD

In her popular novels, such as *The Joy Luck Club* and *The Bonesetter's Daughter*, Chinese American author Amy Tan explores the complicated cultural and social differences between Chinese-born mothers and their American-born daughters. For example, the mothers eat foods and hold religious beliefs that their daughters either abhor or abstain from, while the daughters pursue educational and career opportunities that were not available to the previous generation. Generation gaps occur in almost all families, but as Tan's writings show, such differences are even more pronounced when parents grow up in a different country. When immigrants come to the United States, their initial goal is often to start a new life that is an improvement from the life they experienced in their homeland. However, while these newcomers may intend to fully adapt to American culture, they inevitably bring native customs with them. Immigrants have helped make America broader culturally by introducing new religions, languages, foods, and different ways of looking at the world. Their children and subsequent generations, however, often seek to cast aside these traditions and instead more fully absorb mainstream American mores.

As Tan's writings suggest, the dissimilarities between immigrants and their children are manifested in several ways. Adults who come to the United States and do not learn English turn to their children, educated in the American school system, to serve as interpreters and translators. Children, seeing what their American-born schoolmates eat, reject the foods of their native land. Religion is another area where the generation gap is particularly pronounced. For example, the liturgy of Syrian Christian services had to be translated into English when most young Syrian Americans no longer knew how to speak Syriac. Numerous Jews, freed from the European ghettos they had lived in, wished to assimilate more fully into the surrounding culture and began to loosen the traditional dietary and ritual requirements under which they had grown up. Reformed Judaism, which began in Germany, thus found a strong foothold among young Jews born in America.

However, no generational experiences have been as significant as that between immigrant mothers and their daughters. Living in the United States has afforded girls and young women opportunities they likely would not have had in their homelands. The daughters of immigrants, in some cases, live entirely different lives than their mothers did in their native nations. Where an Arab mother may have only received a limited education, her American-raised daughter enjoys a full course of American public schooling, often continuing on to college and careers. A woman raised in India might have been placed in an arranged marriage, while her daughter will have the opportunity to date and choose a husband. Admittedly, not all families have been willing to give their daughters all these new freedoms, but these American-born girls are frequently more willing to declare their wishes.

The generation gap is only one aspect of the immigrant experience in the United States. Understanding immigrants' unique and shared experiences and their contributions to American life is an interesting way to study the many people who make up the American citizenry. Greenhaven Press's Coming to America series helps readers learn why more people have moved to the United States than to any other nation. Selections on the lives of immigrants once they have reached America, from their struggles to find employment to their experiences with discrimination and prejudice, help give students insights into stereotypes and cultural mores that continue to this day. Finally, profiles of prominent immigrants help the reader become aware of the many achievements of these people in fields ranging from science to politics to sports.

Each volume in the Coming to America series takes an extensive look into a particular immigrant population. The carefully selected primary and secondary sources provide both historical perspectives and firsthand insights into the immigrant experience. Combined with an in-depth introduction and a comprehensive chronology and bibliography, every book in the series is a valuable addition to the study of American history. With immigrants comprising nearly 12 percent of the U.S. population, and their children and grandchildren constantly adding to the population, the immigrant experience continues to evolve. Coming to America is consequently a beneficial tool for not only understanding America's past but also its future.

INTRODUCTION

During the first part of the nineteenth century, the Irish came by the thousands to the United States. Many of these early immigrants were lured by the prospects of jobs. They had few skills when they arrived in the United States, so they took whatever jobs they could get. Usually the working conditions were poor and unsafe and the pay was exceptionally low. However, as the Irish continued to flow into the country, they realized that their sheer numbers, along with their willingness to do work few other Americans would do, gave them a certain amount of power and a voice in the workplace. This realization led them to become involved in America's burgeoning labor movement.

Canal Builders

One of the major drivers of this immigration wave was America's need for cheap labor to build roads and canals. Early leaders such as George Washington had made plans for a network of canals to cross the young nation so that goods and people could be transported more easily. The transportation system became even more necessary following the Louisiana Purchase in 1803, which more than doubled the size of the United States.

One of the first steps toward building a better system of transportation took place in 1817, when the first soil was turned in western New York for the Erie Canal, an ambitious project that would connect Lake Erie with the Atlantic Ocean. At first, local men, many of them farmers during their off-season, worked to clear the land and dig the canal. But when the farmers had to return to their fields, project planners turned elsewhere for cheap labor. One method they used to find workers was to place advertisements in Irish newspapers. Hungry for work and opportunity, thousands of Irish men responded and came to the United States to dig the canal.

The work was difficult, and the young nation had few if any laws prohibiting exploitation of workers. Canal builders faced long days of backbreaking work cutting down trees, pulling stumps, and leveling hills with blasting powder. They lived where they worked, sometimes with their families, in makeshift shacks that were often built on swampy land. Malaria, cholera, typhoid, and other kinds of diseases were rampant. When English novelist Charles Dickens visited America, he toured one of these labor camps and later wrote, "Hideously ugly old women and very buxom young ones, pigs, dogs, men, children, babies, pots, kettles, dung hills, vile refuse, rank straw and standing water, all wallowing together in an inseparable heap, composed the furniture of every dark and dirty hut."[1] Despite the conditions they lived in, the workers protested their working and living conditions only occasionally. In fact, instead of banding together to try to fight for better working conditions, Irish canal workers often divided into factions based on geography or religion, separating themselves into groups of Protestants and Catholics or workers from County Kerry or County Cork. These factions fought over the smallest insults.

Miners

Another kind of work that attracted the Irish in the first half of the nineteenth century was mining. Miners from Scotland, Wales, and England also came to the United States to work, but because there were so many mines in those countries, most of these workers were skilled. Those who emigrated from Ireland, on the other hand, had few if any mining skills, so they were given the most menial or dangerous work.

Regardless of skill level, anyone who entered a mine put his life in danger. Coal and anthracite mines were particularly hazardous. Between 1839 and 1914 at least sixty-one thousand miners died in U.S. coal mines alone. The dangers were many. Miners had to crawl through narrow tunnels, sometimes as deep as a mile or more underground. The heat was intense, and the only light came from candles. Because it was damp, many varieties of fungus grew in the tunnels. Miners breathed in coal dust, and sometimes gasses that formed underground. They also faced danger from cave-ins, fires, floods, and explosions. Often, they had to kneel in water as they extracted coal from the walls of tunnels, and when they had to urinate or defecate, they did so in the tunnels. Miners were also forced to work long hours. One miner wrote:

> [The life of a miner consists of] but to eat his supper . . .
> and then to lie down more like a beast of burden, than a
> being that was made in the image and likeness of his Cre-
> ator. Thus the weary round of life revolves until . . . his
> constitution is completely broken down. . . . He is a mis-
> ery to himself, and a misery to his wife and family, and a
> burden to . . . society. . . . The money he saved has gone
> for doctors. . . . He is probably thirty-five or forty years
> old, but he is past work, an old man.[2]

This was to be the lot of thousands of Irish workers, who labored not only to survive but also in the hope that they could provide a better life for their children. While the overall level of misery increased as more and more Irish came to America, at the same time their increasing numbers became a benefit. During the next decade—the 1840s—hundreds of thousands of Irish immigrants poured into the United States as a result of the Irish

potato famine. By the 1850s more than a million people
had emigrated from Ireland to the United States. While
few of them realized it at the time, it was during these two
decades that Irish Americans began to achieve power in the
workplace; there were so many of them working at jobs
few others were willing to do that their services would have
been missed if they had withdrawn them.

Thoughts of Unionizing

By the 1860s Irish American workers began to take an interest in forming labor unions. Unions were not new to the
United States. They were often formed by craftsmen, usually to strike for one particular cause, such as a shorter
work day, then dissolved after the strike. In 1791 carpenters in Philadelphia struck for a ten-hour day and overtime
pay. In 1825 the first all-woman strike occurred in New
York when the United Tailoresses of New York struck for
a ten-hour day.

But unions for those who performed the most menial
jobs had been rare. The Irish, joined by another immigrant
group that was beginning to grow, the Germans, became
instrumental in establishing the first unions for workers
employed at menial jobs. In the 1860s angry, frustrated
workers began turning on their bosses, sometimes even
killing them, such as in 1863, when a coal operator who
had given a list of his employees to a draft officer was
found murdered. They also went on strike. In 1859, for example, angry Irish laborers in Jersey City, New Jersey, bar-
ricaded railroad tracks they had just laid because they had
not been paid their promised wages. Several of the laborers were given prison terms for their part in the strike, and
they were all labeled by the press a "mongrel mass of ignorance and crime and superstition" and as "utterly unfit
for the common courtesies and decencies of life."[3]

One Irish immigrant who was successful in forming a

union was John Siney, who established the Workingmen's Benevolent Association (WBA) in 1868. The goal of the union was improved working conditions in mines. Siney wanted to affect change through negotiation, not violence, but mine owners did not want to work with the union. They claimed the union was being controlled by the violent Molly Maguires, a secret organization with roots in Ireland.

The Molly Maguires

The Molly Maguires were a group of men with Irish roots who became infamous for violent acts, even acts of terrorism, in the coal and anthracite mines of Pennsylvania. At the time they were active, in the 1860s and 1870s, working conditions were poor, and labor unions were just beginning to be formed. The Molly Maguires were known to have controlled, or at least worked from within, the legal organization The Ancient Order of Hibernians, and were accused of being involved with the WBA, as well.

While historical facts about the Molly Maguires are murky, they are known to have fought against bad working conditions by inflicting terror on—and sometimes murdering—just about anyone in a position of power, including police officers, mine supervisors, and mine owners, and they threatened anyone who was known to have spoken out against them. In 1873 a wealthy coal and railroad magnate named Franklin B. Gowen hired Irishman James McParlan to go undercover and infiltrate the Molly Maguires. In the end McParlan's work resulted in many members of the group being tried for murder and found guilty. Twenty members were hanged, and the Molly Maguires dissolved. According to writer Priscilla Long, however, "The convictions in the Molly Maguire cases were based on flimsy and highly contradictory evidence."[4]

Coal miners and railroad workers were not finished protesting poor working conditions, however. As the Molly

Maguires were being tried, workers were forming unions that gained in strength. In 1873 John Siney left the Workingmen's Benevolent Association to become head of the National Miners' Association, which, unlike the WBA, was against the use of strikes to solve labor disputes. By 1876, however, both the WBA and the NMA had been crushed by mine owners and operators, and in 1880 Siney died of black lung disease, most likely contracted in the mines.

Kate Mullaney

Irish American women also had a hand in forming or supporting some of the earliest American unions. One example of an Irish American woman who worked for better labor conditions is Kate Mullaney. She lived in Troy, New York, where she worked in a commercial laundry, laboring twelve to fourteen hours a day washing, starching, and ironing shirts, collars, and cuffs. She and her coworkers had to plunge their hands into boiling, chemical-filled hot water, and they were often burned by the heavy irons and starch machines. Mullaney was only nineteen when she decided to take action and form a union for women similar to the unions for men she had heard about. She knew that if the three thousand women who worked in Troy's laundry industry would join together, they could be a powerful voice against the dangerous conditions they were forced to confront each day at work.

Organizing the union was difficult. After their long days at work the women were exhausted, and many had families at home to tend to. Many of them were also afraid that if they spoke out against management they would lose their jobs. In 1864, however, Mullaney was successful in forming the first all-female union in the United States, the Collar Laundry Union, with three hundred original members. The women went on strike to get a wage increase and improved working conditions. The strike lasted six days, and in the end the workers' demands were satisfied. Mullaney went on to work on labor issues. She attended the annual meeting of the National Labor Congress in New York City in 1868, where she was named assistant secretary, and she supported workers' rights until her death in 1906.

Mother Jones

Another woman who worked tirelessly for the rights of workers was Irish American Mary Harris Jones, who was known by the name Mother Jones. Jones experienced great tragedy as a young woman when her husband and four children died from yellow fever in 1867. She then worked as a dressmaker but lost her shop to a fire in 1871. Jones had become interested in the labor movement earlier because her husband belonged to a union, but after the fire she began to attend meetings of a union called the Knights of Labor, which was becoming the largest union in the United States. Jones became particularly interested in the plight of miners, and she traveled from mine to mine, living with workers in tents or shacks. She supported the workers during strikes, and for many years she traveled throughout the country holding educational meetings, helping workers understand their rights, and providing information to them about unions.

In the 1890s Mother Jones became an organizer for the United Mine Workers of America. She resigned that position in 1904 and became a lecturer for the Socialist Party of America, touring the country and speaking. But she continued to visit miners and other workers, and she also became involved with children who were forced to work. In 1903 she led a group of children who worked in textile mills on a foot parade from Kensington, Pennsylvania, to the home of President Theodore Roosevelt on Long Island, New York, to protest the conditions that the children labored under. In 1912 she led a parade of miners' children through the streets of Charleston, West Virginia, to publicize their plight. Jones continued to press for workers' rights, participating in strikes by garment workers, streetcar workers, and steel workers, as well as miners. She was greatly loved by those she supported. In reaction to her support of a 1903 miners' strike in Trinidad, Colorado, a local labor newspaper wrote, "This brave little woman has won for herself a simple appellation, the most loving and endearing that the human tongue or pen of man ever couched in the language of a word, 'Mother.'"[5] The *Rocky Mountain News* wrote "Nearly all the miners recognized Mother Jones and took off their hats to her, saluting her with vive Mother Jones."[6] She worked into her nineties and is known as a great figure in American labor history.

The Knights of Labor

One labor union that Irish Americans became involved in was the Noble Order of the Knights of Labor, which was formed in 1869. The labor union claimed to include all working people of all races, along with women, with the exception of professionals such as doctors and lawyers. However, at first Irish Americans did not feel comfortable in the Knights of Labor because the union incorporated ceremonies from the Freemasons, an anti-Catholic secret society that originated in Scotland, in its meetings.

In 1881 the Knights of Labor became more inclusive when Irish American Terence V. Powderly, who had served three terms as mayor of Scranton, Pennsylvania, became its leader. Powderly ended the organization's secrecy and replaced the Masonic-inspired ceremonies with a more generic code of honor, leading many more people to become members. He disliked strikes and was quoted as saying that workers should "have patience and become organized before launching out on strikes, but it is the old story over again. Strike in a hurry and repent at leisure."[7] Powderly turned the union into one with a philosophy of inclusion, and it soon became the largest in the country. However, when immigrants from eastern Europe began to flow into the United States in the last part of the nineteenth century, Powderly worried that they would compete with already established workers for jobs, and he tried to find ways to stop them from gaining employment. The new industries that were cropping up all over the nation needed workers, however, and like the Irish immigrants of the mid–nineteenth century, these new immigrants were willing to do almost any job. With so many new immigrants willing to work for less pay than already established American workers, the Knights began to lose power.

Later Labor Leaders

Irish American labor leaders continued the fight for workers' rights into the twentieth century. John Mitchell, the son of poor Irish immigrants living in Illinois, became the president of the United Mine Workers of America in 1898, and under his leadership union membership swelled from thirty-four thousand to three hundred thousand. Communications Workers of America president Joseph A. Beirne served in that role from 1947 until his death in 1974; before that, he was president of the National Federation of Telephone Workers and negotiated the first national agreement with AT&T. Thomas Kennedy went to work in a coal mine when he was eleven years old and rose to become the president of the United Mine Workers of America in 1960.

Irish immigrants and their children forged the way for other immigrant groups, providing a role model for how to succeed in America with hard work and persistence. Their involvement in labor issues, particularly those relating to low-paying and menial jobs, began primarily out of necessity—too many of them were literally dying from hard work—but soon evolved into a political cause not only to benefit the Irish but all laborers in America. Like so many immigrants in America, the Irish dreamed of a better life, and through their own hard work and activism often obtained their goals while simultaneously shaping their adopted nation.

Notes

1. Quoted in Ronald Takaki, *A Different Mirror: A History of Multicultural America*. Boston: Little, Brown, 1993, p. 147.
2. Quoted in Priscilla Long, *Where the Sun Never Shines*. New York: Paragon House, 1989, p. 62.
3. Quoted in Kerby Miller and Paul Wagner, *Out of Ireland: The Story of Irish Emigration to America*. Washington, DC: Elliott & Clark, 1994, p. 53.
4. Long, *Where the Sun Never Shines*, p. 112.
5. Quoted in Long, *Where the Sun Never Shines*, p. 221.
6. Quoted in Long, *Where the Sun Never Shines*, p. 221.
7. Quoted in Long, *Where the Sun Never Shines*, p. 46.

CHAPTER 1

Leaving Ireland

The First Irish Immigrants

Nelson J. Callahan and William F. Hickey

In this article about America's early Irish immigrants, Nelson J. Callahan and William F. Hickey describe the hard life of a canal worker. They explain that the first immigrants from Ireland came in small numbers and settled along the eastern seaboard. However, when the American government decided to expand the nation's infrastructure in the early nineteenth century—particularly canals and railroads—large numbers of immigrants began arriving from Ireland, attracted by the jobs advertised in Irish newspapers and mentioned in letters from fellow immigrants already settled in the United States. Once on the job, however, the immigrants discovered that the work was harder than they ever imagined and that the living conditions and job-related illnesses were sometimes even worse. Callahan is a Catholic priest and scholar and the author of several books and articles. Hickey is a journalist and freelance writer.

The first record of Irish on American soil, other than those unfortunate women and children who were sent by [Oliver] Cromwell[1] to amuse the planters of Virginia, is marked in the log of the year 1654. Quite appropriately as things turned out, the Irishman's entry to the new world

---

1. Oliver Cromwell, a member of Parliament, overthrew the British monarchy in 1654 and made himself Lord Protector of England; the monarchy was restored in 1660.

was made possible by a ship called "The Goodfellow," which deposited 400 of them on the docks at Boston. No doubt, they preferred the wilds of the unknown continent to their expected treatment at the hands of Cromwell.

The occasion of the landing of this "horde" of Irishmen sent the Yankee natives into a state of outrage and they immediately called for laws that would prevent a repetition of what had occurred. No welcome mat for the Irish in America, but then, what else was new? They weren't even welcome in their own country, so there was no point in going back. They were here and they intended to stay, no matter how the Yankees felt about it.

Stay they did, despite the continued railing of the Bostonian proper and otherwise. They clung like so many barnacles to the wharves and pilings along the waterfront. To say that they prospered would be to stretch truth to the breaking point, but they did multiply, and 83 years after setting foot on American soil, they staged the first St. Patrick's Day parade this country ever witnessed. Needless to say, there has been a Paddy's Day parade down Boston's streets since that eventful March 17, 1737.

From the time "The Goodfellow" first "greened" America, the Irish came steadily to these shores. They did not come in large numbers like their brothers of the Famine, but in a trickle. The nation's first census in 1790 showed that 44,000 Irish lived here. Enough numbers of them had taken root by the time of the Revolutionary War that their presence was felt, and appreciably so by the colonists opposing the dictates of [English king] George III.

Students of history should be aware that the most common surname in the Continental Army was not, as one would imagine Smith or Jones, but Kelly. There were, to be exact, 696 men named Kelly in the ranks of George Washington's inelegant but feisty army. What contribution did they make? Let Washington's adopted son Custis tell it:

*The aid we received from Irish Catholics in the struggle
for independence was essential to our ultimate success.
In the War of Independence, Ireland supplied 100 men
for every single man by any other foreign nation. Let
America bear eternal gratitude to Irishmen.*

America, of course, was not quite ready to go that far,
for the Irish were, after all, Papists [Catholics] to the core
and therefore a threat to the nation's pursuit of liberty and
Protestant approach to life. The Irish would bear watching, and the best method of facilitating that would be to
keep them in their place—in the inner city ghettos. The
Irish, with enough exceptions to prove the rule, kept their
place. They also kept these things close to their hearts, and
the collective organ continued to smolder.

Living Conditions

The conditions under which the Irish lived in the larger
cities along the eastern seaboard were nearly, but not quite,
as wretched as those they sought to escape from in their
homeland. It was a cruel case of poverty and disease, followed by more poverty and disease. There was no work too
menial for them to do and they did it. Despite the dreadful day-to-day existence they suffered, they saved what pen-
nies they could and sent for brothers and sisters back in
Ireland. That action alone gives one a remote clue as to
what life was like in that "Little Black Rose of a Country"
across the sea.

The typical Irish boarding house was a brick building
three to six stories high that was filled "with runners and
shoulderhitters" that preyed on the inhabitants. These ruffians, who worked out of the mandatory grog shop [saloon]
on the first floor, all spoke with brogues and spent their
days either flim-flamming or strongarming the vulnerable
newly-arrived. Yet life was still better here than at home.

Those just off the boat would be taken to one of these

tenements and afforded space in the basement or "bag room." Whole families would be piled atop one another in these dank cellars until death or some other horror emptied a room upstairs. Then the newly-arrived would be allotted one room that, more often than not, would be without ventilation of any sort and would reek with the stench of the previous family's filth. Welcome to America.

A New York cotton buyer, who had just returned from a trip through the South, wrote in 1801: "The Negro slave on the plantations of the South lives under better conditions than most of the Irish in New York. He is also treated more kindly." However true that might have been at the time, the downtrodden Irishman of the big city ghetto had a lot more going for him than the slaves in the South. Foremost, he was a free man, free to move about whatever his economic deprivation. Thus he was allowed to struggle, and that is all the Irishman ever wanted out of life. Let all the cotton buyers in New York lament his condition, the Irish were no slaves.

Besides, the Irishman had his first-floor grog shop where he could gather with his friends and display his sense of humor and social amiability, "shoulder-hitters" or not. Every such "Little Dublin" had social clubs that were usually given names that showed the Irishman was well aware of his status in the new country. There were, for example, a good number of clubs with the title of "The Far Downs."

Mass Migration

The first sizable immigration to America came in 1816, when 9,000 Irish men and women made the crossing. In 1818, when the number doubled, vessels began to be chartered specifically for the purpose of transporting Irish immigrants. They came to be sorely needed, because by the year 1832 some 65,000 souls boarded them, heading for these shores.

Often these Irish were debarked in Canada, either at New Brunswick or Quebec, since many of the first waves of Irish came on Canadian lumber ships, the owners of which saw in those Irish bodies a suitable return cargo. It was profitable for both parties—the ship owners made money and the Irish found it an easy matter to enter the United States. It wasn't difficult to walk across the border, and the Canadian debarkees soon gave New England a Celtic look. In a few decades they would take control of the once Yankee stronghold.

It should also be noted that the mass migration of Irish was more than welcomed by the English, both at home and in Ireland. They saw in that movement a lessening of the "Irish problem." One London newspaper ran an editorial headlined "Good Riddance," which went on to say that "the departing Irish were marauders whose lives were profitably spent in shooting Protestants from behind hedges." It went on to describe the emigrants with such choice words as "vermin," "snakes," "scum" and "demons of assassination.". . .

Moving West: The Erie Canal

The ghetto Irish came to realize that they had to leave the rat-infested tenements in which they dwelled, in order to survive. The death rate among them was horrendous even for those days of primitive medicine, but even more than that, they had no future in a place where a dozen men applied for every job that opened up.

The Irishman's first chance to escape the ghetto was provided by a man named DeWitt Clinton, who as Governor of New York, championed the cause of the Erie Canal and turned the first shovelful of dirt himself in 1817. The Erie Canal, a dream 368 miles long, stretching from Rome, New York, on the Hudson River to Buffalo on Lake Erie, a bridal ribbon of water that would marry the Atlantic Ocean and the Great Lakes, afforded the Irish of the eastern seaboard a chance to push inland, to breathe fresh air. Later, the expansions of the railroads would do the same for other Irishmen, but for now, the Canal would suffice.

The Irish in New York and from as far away as Boston and Baltimore came pouring out of their tenements at the first sign-up call. So many were to follow the original 3,000 signees that they made the digging of the big ditch a private Paddy [a nickname given to Irishman] affair. The work was back-breaking, the pay low and the living conditions poor. So what else was new? A job was a job and the Irishman couldn't afford to be choosy.

As noted, there were so many Irishmen involved in the digging of the Erie Canal that all the canal workers, whatever their national origin, were called either "Longfords" or "Corkonians," depending upon from which area in Ireland the majority of the workers in a given encampment came. According to one digger, however, there was one plus factor about the work—it was the first time an employer in America hadn't lied to an Irishman. The work, indeed, was back-breaking, the pay low and living conditions poor.

Just clearing the adjoining towpaths was difficult enough, but the digging of the canal itself was something else again. The Erie was an ambitiously planned ditch. It was to be 40 feet wide at surface level, sloping to a width of 28 feet at the bottom of its four-foot depth. When one fashions such a ditch 368 miles long, it means that a great deal of dirt has to be moved—megatons of it.

Conditions for Canal Workers

In return for their labor, the canal diggers received 30 [cents] a day for 12 hours on the job, plus board and lodging. The board consisted of coffee and hardtack, with a little sowbelly (bacon) for breakfast, a lunch of bacon, bread and beans, and a dinner of stew, in which the potatoes outweighed the meat. While the meat was often maggoty, the potatoes were always good, and what more could an Irishman ask for, other than a good jigger of whiskey at day's end. Whiskey was, of course, part of any labor contract involving Irishmen, even those negotiated in the cities.

As far as the lodging was concerned, the diggers were provided with army tents, circa War of 1812. It was true the tents were of good size, but they were hardly comfortable, especially when a dozen men were crammed into each one. The canvas abodes were suffocating in summer and icebox cold in winter. In spring it was said that a man could easily drown in one. But oh, those lovely autumn days, those golden, hazy days of late September and early October—they made life worth living.

The Westward-Ho Irishmen soon discovered it was not the wear and tear on their back muscles that was dangerous, but the wear and tear on their insides by creatures they knew nothing about. They were called microbes by the people who knew about such things, and very few people did. Those invisible creatures came to be highly respected, if not feared, for they disabled more Irishmen than all the lower back spasms ever suffered by men the world over.

The deadliest microscopic foe was left by the mosquito, that pesky creature whose sacs dripped with malaria juices. There were, of course, no men the likes of Colonel William Crawford Gorgas, who eradicated the yellow fever among those who dug the Panama Canal in the early 20th Century. The Irish were left to their own devices—a daily jigger of whiskey and rosary beads. Sad to say, neither proved adequate for the occasion and hundreds of diggers went to their eternal reward at an early age from the banks of the Erie Canal.

The second microbic foe caused diarrhea, which while not as deadly, was nevertheless debilitating to an extreme degree. There is simply no way a man can perform hard labor 12 hours at a stretch if his intestines are water-logged. There is an accompanying weakness, not only of the body, but of the mind that prevents a man from exerting his will. Most of the contractors on the Erie Canal, good Christian gentlemen all, could not see the necessity for paying wages for no work. They opted to dock a man's pay.

There was yet another microbe who regularly visited the canal sites, whose sole purpose of existence was to disrupt the Irishman's work habits. It was the germ latter-day physicians would label *diplocoecus pneumoniae*. About 75 varieties of pneumococci are known, and the Irish working on the Erie managed to catch most of them. Admittedly, bouts with this germ tended to be seasonal affairs, mostly in the winter and early spring, but they were serious enough to send many a Paddy to his grave.

Statistics, at their very best, remain boring. Numbers of Irishmen who died while digging the Erie Canal are boring, for they are merely numbers. The mind, in fact, can accommodate any number or series of numbers of deaths and other tragedies. It is only when those stark figures are personalized that the mind feels uneasy. One worker, Timothy Geohagan by name, wrote to his sister in Ireland, telling her of his life and job in the brave new world. "I don't know, dear Sister, if any of us will survive, but God willing, we will live to see a better day," he wrote from his tent near Utica in 1819, "Six of me tentmates died this very day and were stacked like cordwood until they could be taken away. Otherwise, I am fine."

What is remarkable about the letter is that Timothy Geohagan got someone to write it for him and some historian to punctuate it. Although the canal diggers were largely illiterate, they provided those who could write a steady source of income, for letters from workers streamed across the Atlantic. One such hired writer wrote the following to a friend:

I was writing a letter for this poor Paddy and the Paddy wants me to tell the folks back home that he has meat three times each week. When I asked why he wanted me to write that, seeing as to how he got meat three times a day, the Paddy told me that his folks would have a hard enough time understanding him getting meat three times a week and would think he had gone daft if he told the truth.

Though an inordinate number of Irishmen died beside that 368-mile stretch of water, their passing was no more than a ripple in the construction sea that was the Erie Canal. No sooner would an Irishman be buried in a shallow, unmarked grave than two would apply for his job. In other words, while it might have been a watery trail of tears for some, it was equally a stream of hope and ambition for others.

A Clash Among Canal Workers

David Burr

In this letter written by a canal commissioner named David Burr on December 30, 1835, he describes to Indiana governor Noah Noble a clash between two factions of Irish American workers building the Wabash and Erie Canal. Irish immigrants sometimes separated themselves into clans that were based on their birthplaces. The clans often clashed over such matters as who would get the next job or which clan did more work. The fight Burr describes occurred near Huntington, Indiana, when a disagreement between the Corkonians and the Fardowns came to a head. According to Burr, after a riot broke out between the groups in July 1835, their supervisors made the Corkonians work on the upper part of the canal while the Fardowns worked on the lower part. Anyone who strayed was in danger of being beaten by members of the opposing faction. Eventually the company decided that there was too much trouble and that one of the groups had to be dismissed from work altogether. By the middle of July 1835 things became so bad that Burr felt compelled to call on several local militia companies to help stop the fighting.

Dear Sir:

In conformity with your request in relation to the disturbance amongst the Irish laborers on the Canal, it is proper to state that many persons of the two parties into which they are unfortunately divided, "Corkonians and

David Burr, letter to Governor Noah Noble, December 30, 1835.

Fardowns," had been engaged in those bloody affrays at Williamsport in Maryland and at the "high rocks on the Potomac" within the last two years. They had come since September in 1834 to the Wabash and Erie Canal with, as it is said, many of their leaders. Of course, they had brought their animosities with them. And from that time up to the twelfth of July last, when the general riot took place, they manifested their ill will to each other by merciless beatings on such persons of each party as chanced to fall in the power of each other. On a considerable portion of the line there was no justice of the peace in these newly organized counties. . . .

Trouble on the Line

Because of mutual fears and for the safety of the laborers had so hired to the contractors that they had about equally divided the line between the parties; the Corkmen worked on the upper part, and the Fardowns on the lower part of the line. The beatings of such persons who were caught away from their friends increased to such a degree, and the parties became so exasperated, that about the first of July a determination became general that one or the other should leave the line. The worthless amongst them, by carrying threats of burnings and murders which were to be committed by falling on the defenseless in the night, so excited their fears that they left their houses and cabins and hid out in the woods without light or fire to betray their hiding places. The whole line, armed in military array, worked generally in the daytime until some idle report would get in circulation that one party was marching to fight the other. Then they would leave their work and hasten with great rapidity to the supposed point of danger.

From the fourth to the tenth of July, these alarms were constant and were aggravated by the threats and outrages of the worthless. The length of line occupied by these belligerent parties was nearly fifty miles. On the tenth of July the parties hastily collected, or rather, they left their work and commenced a march towards the center of the line for a general battle. . . .

I then went to the reputed battlefield with three or four persons whom I supposed had influence with them. I found them fully prepared, well disposed in a strong military position, and exceedingly exasperated; and I had some difficulty in saving those who went with me from being killed. They expressed the same fears as the others but, after some persuasion, consented to appoint persons to agree on terms of peace with the Fardowns. They also agreed to suspend hostile operations until the result of the meetings between the persons deputized to negotiate the peace could be known.

The Militia Is Called In

In the meantime, the citizens of Huntington had become exceedingly alarmed at seeing this hostile array; three or four hundred armed men on each side had the avowed intention of meeting in battle; the civil authority was completely powerless. Fearing their persons and property would not be safe, they sent to Fort Wayne for aid of the militia. A company immediately was collected and in a few hours was sent to their relief. Meanwhile, the citizens of Huntington had collected and organized a company also.

By this time, the citizens of Lagro had become alarmed; they sent to Huntington for the troops to come and protect them and aid the civil authority. As soon as I learned the militia had turned out from sixty to one hundred in number, I thought the force altogether too small to do any good against seven hundred armed men. Therefore, I sent to Logansport and requested assistance, which was promptly rendered. The militia at Lagro, at my request marched to Miamisport and met two volunteer companies from Logansport; and all marched back to Lagro.

Two magistrates, an associate judge, the sheriffs of Huntington and Wabash counties, and the militia arrested and committed eight of the ringleaders. There was no safe jail on the canal line. Therefore, in order to remove the cause of contention, these men were sent under a strong guard to Indianapolis for safekeeping. Here they were confined until they were liberated by a writ of habeas corpus because of some informality in the proceedings.

With great respect,
David Burr

Fleeing from Famine

Judy Ball

In this selection Judy Ball, managing editor of *Millennium Monthly* and *American Catholic Online*, provides the background for the events that led to the mass emigration from Ireland in the 1840s. She explains that the political and socioeconomic climate that had been in place since the sixteenth century set the stage for what would become a disaster when a fungus first hit the potato crop in 1845. Because millions of people in Ireland relied upon potatoes for sustenance, the resulting crop failure brought on not only starvation and sickness but also began what would become a flood of immigrants to the United States.

With the benefit of hindsight, social historians can now offer convincing evidence that significant portions of rural Ireland in the 1840's were ripe for trouble. Indeed, ominous social undercurrents had been churning for hundreds of years, beginning with what Dr. [Donal] McCartney [Professor Emeritus of History at University College Dublin] calls Britain's ultimately successful "conquest of Ireland" dating from the 16th century.

By confiscating Irish-owned land and "planting" the island with Protestant English and Scottish landlords, the British introduced a new landed class politically loyal to the Empire. The social gulf and the divided political and religious loyalties between landlord and worker would only grow over the centuries to come.

The Penal Laws of the late 17th century forbidding

Judy Ball, "The Famine That Brought the Irish to America," *St. Anthony Messenger*, www.catholic.org, November 1997. Copyright © 1997 by St. Anthony Messenger Press and Franciscan Communications. Reproduced by permission.

Catholics to own, purchase or inherit land left a bitter taste. Then, in 1800, came the Act of Union that officially abolished the independent Irish Parliament in Dublin; henceforth the British Parliament supervised affairs from London.

The disappearance of Ireland's own Parliament is no idle historical point of interest, says Dr. Kevin Whelan, research scholar with the Royal Irish Academy in Dublin. It means, he says carefully, that "the Famine [of 1845–1850] did not occur in Ireland, but in the United Kingdom of Great Britain and Ireland" that had been created by the Act of Union. But that was not all.

The socioeconomic hierarchy created by the 16th-century "plantation" efforts left landlords, mostly Protestant but some Catholic, at the top of the ladder. Below them were ever smaller farmers, including so-called cottiers who lived in one-room cabins and, on the lowest rung, the utterly vulnerable tenant farmers.

While many of the landlords were absentees living in England or in Dublin's Georgian houses, they or their sub-landlords were only too happy to have their on-site agents parcel out the land in increasingly smaller plots. The landlords' ultimate goal was to get as much rent as they could from as many tenants as possible.

The pre-Famine Irish unwittingly cooperated, marrying early and having large families. The population, which had doubled between 1750 and 1800, doubled yet again in 1841 to just over eight million people. Among them were two million landless laborers. As the population escalated and the gap widened between rich and poor, so did the latter's dependence on the ecological miracle crop of the day: the potato. On the eve of the Famine, approximately 25 percent of the population lived off the potato while another 50 percent were virtually dependent on it for subsistence.

Poverty, Population, Potatoes

Then, in 1845, came reports of potatoes going black in some fields. One third of the crop was lost. What was dismissed by some as "just a bad year" was followed in 1846 and again in 1847 by a decline in three quarters of the potato crop. The potato fungus (*phytophthora infestans*) which had migrated in the late 1500's from Peru and ultimately moved from the United States to Europe, had planted itself deeply and disastrously in the Irish soil.

"The cruelty of the timing of the Famine," says Dr. Whelan, "was that it came precisely when the economic and demographic curves were most out of synch." The irony continued. In response to the disaster, impoverished farmers sold any cash crops they could, becoming ever more dependent on the potato.

Suddenly, unmistakably, Ireland was facing the worst famine in European history. The odor of decaying potatoes pervaded the land. Hardest hit was the vast impoverished underclass, outwitted by three potent enemies: poverty, population and the diseased potato.

Increasingly gruesome realities haunted the tiny island which soon was overrun with hunger and disease. What few farm animals there were died off. People sold their boats to buy food and ate the following year's seed potatoes. Entire families desperately turned to anything they could consume, including grass, in a futile effort to stay alive.

Food riots erupted as people saw grains and other foods being exported or grew impatient for long-awaited relief works. Typhus and cholera were rampant, inducing a fear and dread not experienced since the Black Death in the Middle Ages. Dead bodies rotted in fields and along roadsides, or were eaten by rats and dogs. Entire families succumbed to famine and disease behind their cottage doors in a final attempt to preserve a sense of privacy and dignity.

In the end, some made their final journey to mass

graves on carts stacked high with bodies. Still others were transported via hinged coffins which, ingeniously and insidiously, could be used time and again.

The Irish and the British and, indeed, the world, were caught off guard and scrambled to respond. A number of temporary relief programs were immediately introduced by the British to alleviate the suffering. Donated food arrived, often at the initiation of Irish-Americans. British Prime Minister Sir Robert Peel made arrangements for Indian corn (maize) to be imported from the United States. Even those who were alarmed at the growing disaster misread the scope and strength of what would prove to be a five-year assault on the Irish economy, to say nothing of the Irish spirit.

Added to that, says Dr. Whelan, was the pre-Famine

Peasants seize the potato crop of an evicted tenant. During the potato blight, Irish families struggled to survive.

British conviction that the Irish were "Celtic" and "other," that they were "papists who were backward and primitive and who needed to be fast-forwarded into civilization. The British saw the potato as a root crop for a primitive people." Furthermore, the notion of so-called providentialism was powerful at the time. People who held to it, Dr. Whelan explains, believed that "the Famine would do permanent good out of transient evil. . . . God was delivering a signal to Ireland, and they should not interfere too much with the will of God." They included Charles Trevelyan, who served during the Famine as assistant secretary of the treasury and had major responsibility for relief efforts.

Meanwhile, the predominant laissez-faire economic policy (meaning "let be") held that it was simply not government's job to interfere with the free market or to provide aid for its citizens; people were to be self-sufficient, and charity would only weaken them.

Safety Nets Destroyed

The response to the Famine was a patchwork of on-again, off-again relief programs too often administered with a when-is-this-ever-going-to-end attitude. These included so-called workhouses for the utterly destitute but which, in fact, became punitive, oppressive and disease-ridden facilities dreaded by all but the most desperate.

Works programs designed to employ men at such tasks as building public roads faltered for many reasons, including halfhearted support on the part of landowners as well as greed and inefficiency. As the crops failed again in 1846 and food prices rose higher, an increasing number of people, often starving, were employed building roads which often led nowhere or were located in deserted areas where they were not needed. As more and more men scrambled to earn a little money—if they had the energy to work—millions more were succumbing to starvation.

Soup Kitchens

The Soup Kitchen Act of early 1847 sought to replace the overburdened relief works system with temporary feeding facilities. The kitchens were to function only briefly, until the harvest in September offered relief. Meanwhile, the number of people engaged in relief work was drastically cut even before the soup kitchens had been established. In some areas, angry, despairing crowds demanded work and rejected the idea of queuing in public for food that, in many cases, was of such poor quality that it offered little nutrition.

A small number of privately run soup kitchens engaged in "souperism," distributing food to people only if they promised to give up the Catholic faith and become Protestant, or trying to induce the masses by serving meat-filled soup on Fridays, when Catholics were still forbidden to eat meat.

Still, some of the official relief programs worked miracles, extending if not saving lives. Also, the St. Vincent de Paul Society sprang into action. Particularly noble and successful efforts were made by the Quakers, who numbered only 3,000 out of a population of more than 8 million. Still, they succeeded in saving many lives through their organized distribution of food and their refusal to proselytize. "We will never know how many lives were saved as a result" of these efforts, says Rob Goodbody, a member of the History Committee of the Society of Friends, "but in the folk memory of Ireland, Quakers are known as people who helped during the Famine."

By the time the soup kitchens were closed in September 1847, three million people had been fed each day, but the systems that had been put into place grew less effective while the desperate masses grew weaker. Famine and disease overrode the land, and large numbers of poor tenant farmers were evicted from their small plots of land.

Evicted families took shelter wherever they could, including roadside ditches. Others lurched to the nearest workhouse if it was not too distant and if room was available. A limited number of the evicted were given a small sum of money by their landlords for the purpose of emigrating. While these landlords were initially praised for their generosity, the practice soon came to be seen as enforced exile—nothing like the pre-Famine emigration among the mostly young and strong who were leaving Ireland by choice. The estimated 1.2 million people who emigrated in 1846–52 were further induced by newspaper ads and placards urging them to leave.

Substandard Ships

They certainly were in no position to be selective about the conditions under which they traveled. Many of the so-called coffin ships, often unseaworthy, were stuffed with humans themselves unfit for the difficult journey. An unknown number died at sea as the sick and the healthy were cooped up together for weeks on overcrowded ships with unsanitary conditions, rotten food and foul water. Typhus was so prevalent it became known as "ship fever."

Those who crossed the Atlantic more likely landed in Canada, which charged lower fares and which offered more relaxed immigration rules than did the United States. But most of those who survived the weeks at sea and successfully passed through the quarantine station ultimately headed for the United States—by the back door, if necessary. "The immigrants were lemmings rushing to America, and nothing was going to stop them," says Joseph Robins, a retired social historian in Dublin.

Americans did not readily welcome what they saw as hordes of impoverished and diseased immigrants unfit for almost any kind of work. Still, the new arrivals flocked to the large cities, where they lived in slum areas and picked up work as unskilled labor. Only 10 percent headed to the familiar rural areas in search of a life with which they had been familiar in Ireland. The land had betrayed them once; the fear was that it just might happen again.

How Emigration Affected Ireland

Back in Ireland, the Famine continued with a vengeance and the torrent of emigration continued. By 1850 the worst was over and the potato crop had recovered some of its strength. But some provinces within Ireland had lost 25 percent of their populations to starvation and disease, with three fifths of the deaths among children under 10 and adults over 60.

The other losses were harder to calculate, but of equally staggering dimensions. "No modern historian would argue the case for genocide," says Kevin Whelan, but the Famine was certainly "ethnocidal" in that it "led to the destruction of a culture" and the "unraveling" of so much of what had been. "The Famine," he says, "ripped gaping holes in the moral membranes of Irish society, leaving only the biological husk. It was a bomb that left demographic shrapnel."

Bonds between people had come apart. Solidarity, neighborliness, the safety nets of Irish life were destroyed. The Irish experience of death, once a communal affair, was replaced by a "numbness," according to Whelan. People were "isolated" and "devoid of direction, drained of hope." There was a pervasive "sense of sadness and despondency in the culture." Even the Irish language came close to dying out: Of the estimated 1.2 million who died, three quarters of them spoke Gaelic, as did a significant number of emigrants. The Irish language was "increasingly marginalized." It came to be "something which belonged to the private world, to family, to home only."

Dangerous and Unpleasant Departures

Anonymous

The following article was published in the *Illustrated London News* on May 10, 1851, six years after the first appearance of the fungus that destroyed Ireland's potato crop. By 1851 more than a million people had immigrated—most of them to the United States—and more than a million more had died in Ireland of starvation or disease. The newspaper's correspondent from Cork, Ireland, describes the ordeal immigrants went through as they left the only homes most of them had ever known and tried to get passage on board immigrant ships. Before they could begin their transatlantic voyage, these immigrants were often obliged to stay in crowded boardinghouses in Cork, Dublin, and other port cities. Because of the close living quarters and filthy conditions, many immigrants died of diseases before they could depart Ireland.

The Census Returns, when published, will enable us to ascertain, in some degree, the extent of the combined ravages of famine and pestilence, in the first place, and of despair and emigration, in the second, in the depopulation of Ireland. But even these returns, authentic as they will be, cannot be complete; for the emigration that has gone on since the census was taken, and which still continues, will compel the statist to make large deductions from the amount which the census will yield, if he wish to ascertain the real number of the Irish people. The annals of the

Anonymous, "The Depopulation of Ireland," *Illustrated London News*, May 10, 1851.

modern world offer no such record as that presented in the history of Ireland, since the memorable and deplorable years of the potato famine, and of the pestilence that followed in its track. The splendid emigrant ships that ply between Liverpool and New York, and which have sufficed in previous years to carry to the shores of America an Irish emigration, amounting on the average to 250,000 souls per annum, have, during the present spring, been found insufficient to transport to the States the increasing swarms of Irish who have resolved to try in the New World to gain the independence which has been denied them in the old.

"Emigration," says a letter dated a few days back, "is proceeding to an extent altogether unprecedented: but much less, in proportion, from Ulster than the other provinces. From most of the southern counties, the small farmers are hastening in vast numbers; and even in Leinster the mania for emigration prevails far and wide. The remittances from America are far greater in amount than in any previous year, and considerable sums are paid by the banks and by private commercial establishments, from day to day, on orders from the United States. From some districts in Ulster, numbers of the smaller tenantry are taking their departure. From one of the principle estates in Monaghan nearly one thousand persons of the cottier class are about to be sent to Canada at the expense of the landlord, who, it is stated, has made arrangements for providing them with a comfortable passage, and some small allowance of money to each family after reaching the port of their destination."

The number of emigrant vessels proceeding to America direct from Irish ports is quite unprecedented, and is one of the most extraordinary circumstances of the time. Within eight days, the following eleven vessels, carrying 1568 passengers, sailed from the single port of Cork:— The *Dominique*, for Quebec, 150 passengers; the *Don*, for

New York, 160; the *Lockwoods*, for New York, 280; the *Marchioness of Bute*, for Quebec, 120; the *Sara*, for Boston, 104; the *Solway*, for New York, 196; the *Try Again*, for Quebec, 130; the *Favourite*, for Boston, 120; the *Clarinda*, for New York, 100; the *Swift*, for Boston, 120; the *Field Marshal Radetzsky*, for New York, 88 passengers. In addition to those vessels, the *Hotspur* went down the Cork river, on Tuesday, with 100 paupers on board, from the Kenmare Union-house.

Eviction of Tenants

But what is most remarkable is, that, while this enormous emigration is going on, leading to a fear in some parts of the country that sufficient people will not be left to cultivate the land, the owners or mortgagees of Irish estates continue to evict their tenantry with as much virulence as ever. The *Galway Vindicator* states:—"There were 195 ejectments entered—13 at the suit of the trustees of A.H. Lynch, one of Mathew S. Coneys, and 181 were brought by the Law Life Insurance Company; and of 183 entries of civil bills, 87 were at the suit of the insurance company. With the exception of three or four, the ejectments were all undefended. They were disposed of at the rate of one each minute; so that, taking an average of five souls to each family ejected, we will have 300 per hour, and in the entire 905 human beings cast upon poor-house relief."

The same journal estimates the total evictions in Connemara during the present season at upwards of 4000. In Limerick and Kerry the same system is carried on; the evicted remaining in the union workhouse until remittances arrive from their friends in America, when they shake from their feet the dust of their native land, and rejoin their friends and relations across the Atlantic.

The following letter from our Correspondent in Cork . . . gives the latest information upon this interesting sub-

ject:—"The constant appearance of the heading 'Emigration from Ireland,' and the no less constant stream of well-
clad, healthy, and comfortable-looking peasantry in our
streets, induces me to send you the accompanying sketches
and communications on that subject.

"Upon reference to notes and papers of my own, and to
information afforded me by the emigration agents here, I
am disposed to think that about the middle of May the
great emigrational torrent ceases to flow from these shores.
Looking backward for the last month, I find that, during
the week ending April 11, the greatest rush for the season
took place. The numbers who left Cork that week could not
have fallen far short of 1500 souls, and this with the emigration of the other ports of Limerick, Waterford, Dublin,
and even of Belfast, will give us an approach to 5000
weekly leaving the country. Large as this number may appear, it is well known that it is considerably below the mark
when the departures for Liverpool are included. One agent
informed me that he himself had booked 600 emigrants in
four days, and yet he is but one of the many agents who are
to be met with not alone in the large towns and seaports,
but even thickly scattered through each petty town and village throughout the country. In England you can have but
little conception of the sufferings of the poor Irish emigrant from the time he first announces his intention of
leaving home to his final departure: nor, indeed, can it be
understood even in this country, except by those who make
it their business to investigate the subject. Impressed with
this belief, and being desirous of witnessing some of the
partings of the emigrants from amidst the scenes of their
youth, I took, a few days since, a run into the south-west of
the country, from whence the great stream pours into the
city of Cork. In my ramble I fell in with a clergyman, who
was there on his way to take leave of a large number of his
parishioners, who were then packing up.

"None perhaps feel more severely the departure of the peasantry than the Roman Catholic clergy; as from them, and them alone, it may be said, comes the sole means of support which they receive. Yet none take a more active part in seeing them safely out of the country, or have looked more closely to the interest of those they leave behind, than those clergymen, even though their revenues are reduced, in most cases, to one-half, and in some to one-third. In company with one of these humble but exemplary men, I came to a sharp turn in the road, in view of that for which we sought, and of which I send you a sketch, namely, the packing and making ready of, I may say, an entire village—for there were not more than half-a-dozen houses on the spot, and all their former inmates were preparing to leave. Immediately that my rev. friend was recognised, the people gathered about him in the most affectionate manner. He had a word of advice to Pat, a caution to Nelly, a suggestion to Mick; and he made a promise to Dan to take care of the 'old woman,' until the five pounds came in the spring to his 'Reverence' to send her over to America. Then ensued a scene of tears and lamentation, such as might have softened a much harder heart than mine or that of the priest. He stood for awhile surrounded by the old and the young, the strong and the infirm, on bended knees, and he turned his moistened eyes towards heaven, and asked the blessing of the Almighty upon the wanderers during their long and weary journey. Many were the tears brushed quietly away from the sunburnt cheeks of those who there knelt, and had implicit faith that the benediction so fervently and piously asked, would be vouchsafed to them.

From Country to City

"It was not pleasant to linger amid a scene like this; so to dispel our sadness, we took a last farewell of the group, and ere long found ourselves upon the road to Kenmare, and in the midst of a train of from 200 to 300 men and women, boys and girls, varying in age from ten to thirty years. They looked most picturesque in their gay plaid shawls and straw bonnets, and were all on their way to Cork, to go on board the emigrant ship.

"Upon inquiry I was given to understand that this was but one of the many groups sent from the union-houses through the country, and at the expense of the ratepayers. This, though an expensive process, is better than to leave them to pine and perish with want, as in the too wretched union of [the town of] Kilrush; yet it is sad to see so much young blood sent from amongst us, and that too, as a gentleman, an extensive farmer in the county of Kerry, told me, at a period when it is found difficult to obtain hands to do the necessary farm-work. To so great an extent has this extraordinary emigration mania been carried in the county of Kerry, that this gentleman told me that he had been obliged even thus early to engage farm labourers at Mill-street, in the county of Cork, to take in his harvest in the county of Kerry during the coming season. Moreover, he stated that he was not the only one in the county who would be obliged to have recourse to the same means of procuring labourers. It would be strange indeed, that Ireland, who, at one time, was able to supply with her superabundant labour the farmers of England and Wales, should be obliged to seek in the English and Welsh fields for hands to do her work. Yet it is quite possible that such a thing may happen.

"Having seen sufficient of the country, I turned my steps towards the city, and upon my arrival there, first sought out the houses of the strangers who frequently are obliged to remain in lodging-houses from one to five or six days, according to circumstances. I can assure you that it is not exaggerating the abject misery of these miscalled 'lodging-houses for emigrants.' It is no unusual thing to thrust from twenty to forty persons, of all ages and both sexes, into rooms not more than four yards by five or six yards square, with no other accommodation than a mass of filthy straw, placed around the room, upon which the weary traveller is expected to find repose. In the event of his being provided by the proprietor with some sort of covering, he is charged threepence a night; should they bring their own bed-clothes, they pay twopence; and those who are content to sleep on the straw, without divesting themselves of the rags, pay one penny.

"For standing room where they may breakfast or dine—for it cannot be called accommodation—the charges are pretty much on the same scale. On the whole, it is fortunate that the great business of emigration is generally over before the setting-in of the warm weather, otherwise these lodging-houses, from their over-crowded state, as well as from the accumulated amount of filth in them, would become perfect nuisances, and dangerous to the health of the community. . . .

Aboard a Ship

"Having thus shown you what was picturesque in the passage of the group of emigrants from the home of their infancy to the office of the emigration agent who provides them with a ship direct from the port, . . . I . . . will readily explain the mode in which those vessels are fitted up, and where each party gets so many square inches to her or his share of ship, as the case may be, and where, if I am given rightly to understand, man, woman, and child are obliged to huddle together like pigs at a fair. But then the ship is partitioned, divided, and formed exactly according to the strict letter of the law, and none can grumble, yet few can go on board one of them without being instantly struck with the chances that appear of the complete demoralization of the whole group; and what it must be when the sea rolls heavily, when the hatches are all closed, and the ship heaves and labours in the storm, can be much better imagined by others than described by me. The answer given to a party who, upon seeing the way in which these unfortunate beings were left to toss and tumble about, asked if even a plank in the shape of a table was not to be provided for them was, 'Cock them up with it, indeed! How badly off they're for a table!' And yet this man is known to be a kind, generous-hearted man in other respects.

"Every inquiry or remonstrance is answered by the allegation, that all is according to the Act of Parliament, or 'the Act so directs it;' so that you will perceive what little chances of extra comforts the emigrant has who emigrates in the smaller vessels belonging to men, some of whom are making lordly fortunes by their new trade.

"Having now shown you so much of what appertains to those who sail from this port direct to America, nothing remains but to [explain] the departure of the steamers for Liverpool, which generally, of late, have been crowded to suffocation, owing, perhaps, as much to the cheapness of the fares, caused by the steam-boat opposition for some time back, as to a previous knowledge among the emigrants that they will be better provided for in the way of a ship in Liverpool, the 'great port of embarkation,' than they are likely to be in Irish vessels.

"The withdrawal of this ruinous competition will now, no doubt, in this matter of emigration, materially serve the Cork Steam-ship Company, as doubtless large numbers of those who heretofore made for Waterford, will be now tempted to turn their thoughts towards Cork, owing to the superiority of the vessels leaving the port. From early dawn on the day of the steamer's sailing up to the hour of starting, whether it be ten in the morning or five in the evening, the curious in those matters will be sure to find the quays leading to the packet-office one continued stream of cars, carts, trucks, and porters, and all heavily laden with feather-beds, boxes, trunks, indescribable baggage and sacks of potatoes, and all tending to the one centre, namely, the deck of the *Nimrod*, and where the well-disposed as also the ill-disposed are sure to congregate to witness the departure. . . .

"During the existence of the low fares, it was more than once stated that 'some of the emigrants were wretched and miserable-looking beings.' At present it is the bone and sinew of the land that appear to go out, and even those in more than comfortable circumstances are often among the number, as the immense sums of money sent into this country from relatives in America (our branch bank alone paid out, on account of remittances received during this season, the large sum of £40,000) testify."

Passages from an 1847 Famine Ship Diary

Robert Whyte

In 1847 Robert Whyte boarded the *Ajax* for Canada. Many Irish immigrants chose to sail to Canada and then make their way to the United States, rather than travel directly, because passage on a Canadian ship was usually cheaper. Whyte wrote an account of his voyage that was published in 1848. In these passages from the diary, he relates the unhealthy conditions on the ship and the illnesses that quickly spread among the passengers.

Sunday, 13 June

The reports from the hold became very alarming and the mistress [ship's nurse] was occupied all day attending the numerous calls upon her. She already regretted having come on the voyage, but her kind heart did not allow her to consult her case. When she appeared upon deck she was beset by a crowd of poor creatures, each having some request to make, often of a most inconsiderate kind and few of which it was in her power to comply with. The day was cold and cheerless and I occupied myself reading in the cabin.

Monday, 14 June

The head committee brought a can of water to show it to the captain it was quite foul, muddy and bitter from having been in a having cask. When allowed to settle it became clear, leaving considerable sediments in the bottom of the

James J. Mangan, ed., *Robert Whyte's 1847 Famine Ship Diary: The Journey of an Irish Coffin Ship*. Dublin: Mercier Press, 1994. Copyright © 1994 by Patrick Conroy. Reproduced by permission.

vessel but it retained its bad taste. Then mate endeavoured to improve it by trying the effect of charcoal and of alum but some of the casks were beyond remedy and the contents, when pumped out, resembled nauseous ditch water. There were now eight cases of serious illness—six of them being fever and two dysentery. The former appeared to be of a peculiar character and very alarming, the latter disease did not seem to be so violent in degree.

The Disease Spread Among Passengers

Tuesday, 15 June

The reports this morning were very afflicting and I felt much that I was unable to render any assistance to my poor fellow passengers. The captain desired the mistress to give them everything out of his own stores that she considered would be of service to any of them. He felt much alarmed, now was it to be wondered at that contagious fever—which under the most advantageous circumstances and under the watchful eyes of the most skillful physicians baffles the highest ability—should terrify one having the charge of so many human beings likely to fall a prey to the unchecked progress of the dreadful disease; for once having shown itself in the unventilated hold of a small brig, containing one hundred and ten living creatures, how could it possibly be stayed without medicines, skill or even pure-water to slake the patients burning thirst?

The prospect before us was indeed an awful one and there was no hope for us but in the mercy of God.

Wednesday, 16 June

The past night was very rough and I enjoyed little rest. No additional cases of sickness were reported, but there were apparent signs of insubordination amongst the healthy men, who complained of starvation and the want of water to make drinks for their sick wives and children. A deputation came aft to acquaint the captain with their grievances but he ordered them away and would not listen to a word from them. When he went below the ringleader threatened that they would break into the provision store.

The mate did not take any notice of the threat but repeated to me, in their hearing, an anecdòte of his own experience, of a captain, showing with what determination he suppressed an outbreak in his vessel. He concluded by alluding to cut-lasses and the firearms in the cabin. And in order to make a deeper impression on their minds, he brought up the old blunderbuss from which be fired a shot, the report of which was equal to that a small cannon. The deputation slunk away muttering complaints.

If they were resolute they might easily have seized upon the provisions. In fact, I was surprised how famished men could so patiently bear with their own and their starved children's sufferings, but the captain would willingly have listened to them if it were in his power to relieve their distress.

Thursday, 17 June

Two new cases of fever were announced and from the representation of the mate, the poor creatures in the hold were in a shocking state. The men who suffered from dysentery were better, the mistress' prescription—flour porridge with a few drops of a laudanum—having given them relief. The requests of the friends of the fever patients were most preposterous some asking for beef, others wine. They were all desirous of landanum being administered to them in order to procure sleep but we were afraid to dispense so dangerous a remedy except with extreme caution.

Our progress was almost imperceptible and the captain began to grow very uneasy, there being at the rate of the already miserable allowance of food, but provisions for 50 days. It also now became necessary to reduce the complement of water and to urge the necessity of using sea water in cookery.

Friday, 18 June

The fireplaces were the scenes of endless contentions. The sufferings they endured appeared to embitter the wretched emigrants one against another. Their quarrels were only ended when the fires were extinguished at 7 p.m. at which time they were surrounded by squabbling groups preparing their miserable evening meal. They would not leave until Jack mounted of the foremast and precipitated a bucket full of water on each fire—when they snatched up their pots and pans and, half blinded by the steam, descended into the hold with their half-cooked suppers. Although Jack delighted in teasing them, they never complained of his pranks, however annoying. . . .

Saturday, 19 June

A shark followed us all the day and the mate said it was a certain forerunner of death. The cabin was like an apothecary's shop and the mistress a perfect slave. I endeavoured to render her every assistance in my power. The mate also was indefatigable in his exertions to alleviate the miserable lot of our helpless human cargo.

Not having seen the stowaway on deck for some time upon inquiring after him, I learned that he was amongst the sick and was very bad but he was kindly attended by the young man from the County Clare who devoted himself to attending the afflicted, some of whom the members of their own families neglected to take care of.

The Misery Continues

Sunday, 20 June

Having hinted to the captain the propriety of having divine service read upon the Sabbath, he said that it could not be done. Indeed the sailors seldom had a spare moment and as to the mate, I often wondered how he got through so much work. This day, therefore, had no mark to distinguish it from any other. The poor emigrants were in their usual squalid attire, neither did the crewing themselves out as on former Sundays.

All were dispirited and a cloud of melancholy hung over us.

The poor mistress depicted that she could not get an opportunity of reading her Bible. I pitied her from my heart knowing how much she felt the distress that surrounded us and her anxiety to lighten the affliction of the passengers.

Monday, 21 June

I was surprised at the large allowance of food served out to the sailors. They had each 1–2 lbs of beef or pork daily, besides coffee and as much biscuit as they pleased, but it being a temperance vessel, they had no grog, in lieu of which they got lime-juice. However, there was a little cask of brandy in a corner of the cabin but the captain was afraid to broach it, knowing the mate's propensity. I noticed the latter often casting a wistful glance at it as he rose from dinner and he did not fail to tell me that it was the best possible preventive against the fever.

Tuesday, 22 June

One of the sailors was unable for duty and the mate feared he had the fever.

The reports from the hold were growing ever more alarming and some of the patients who were mending, had relapsed. One of the women was every moment expected to breathe her last and her friends—an aunt and cousins—were inconsolable about her as they had persuaded her to leave her father and mother and come with them.

The mate said that her feet were swollen to double their natural size and covered with black putrid spots. I spent a considerable part of the day watching a shark that followed in our wake with great constancy. . . .

Tuesday, 6 July

During the past night there was a heavy fall of rain

which left the atmosphere clear and cool.

Two men (brothers) died of dysentery and I was awakened by the noise made by the mate, who was searching for an old sail to cover the remains with. In about an hour after, they were consigned to the deep, a remaining brother being the solitary mourner. He continued long to gaze upon the ocean, while a tear that dropped from his moistened eye told the grief he did not otherwise express. I learned in the afternoon that he was suffering from the same complaint that carried off his brothers.

Wednesday, 7 July

The phosphorescent appearance of the ocean at night was very beautiful. We seemed to be gliding through a sea of liquid fire. We passed a great number of fishing boats, chiefly French, from the isles St. Pierre and Miquelon.

They were anchored at regular intervals for the purpose of catching cod-fish, which, allured by the vast numbers of worms found upon the bottom, abound upon the banks.

The vessels generally are large sloops and have a platform all round with an awning over the deck. When a fish is taken, it is immediately split and cleaned, then it is thrown into the hold and, when the later is full, the fishermen return home and land their cargo to be dried and saved.

Owing to these processes being sometimes too long deferred, the bank fish, though larger, is considered inferior to that taken along the coast of Newfoundland.

Great variety of opinion exists respecting the nature and origin of these submarine banks but none of them appears to me so natural as this. The stream which issues from the Gulf of Mexico, commonly called the 'Florida gulf stream', being checked in its progress by the southern coast of Newfoundland, deposits the vast amount of matter held in suspension. This, by accumulation, formed the banks which are still increasing in extent. The temperature of the water upon the banks is higher than that

of the Gulf of St Lawrence and of the ocean and its evap-
oration causes the fog that almost perpetually prevails.

The afternoon was clear with a gentle breeze which
formed a ripple on the surface of the water and gave a
beautiful appearance to the reflection of the declining sun,
looking like jets of gas bursting from the deep.

Thursday, 8 July

Another of the crew was taken ill, thereby reducing our
hands when they were most required. The captain had a
great dread of the coast of Newfoundland which, being
broken into deep bays divided from each other by rocky
capes, is rendered exceedingly perilous, more especially, as
the powerful currents set towards this inhospitable shore.

We kept a lookout for some vessel coming from the
gulf, in order to learn the bearings of land but did not perceive one during the day.

Friday, 9 July

A few convalescents appeared upon deck. The appearance of the poor creatures was miserable in the extreme.
We now had fifty sick, being nearly one half the whole
number of passengers. Some entire families, being pros-
trated, were dependent on the charity of their neighbours,
many of whom were very kind, but others seemed to be
possessed of no feeling. Among the former, the head committee was conspicuous.

The brother of the two men who died on the sixth instant followed them today. He was seized with dismay from
the time of their death, which no doubt hurried on the
malady to its fatal termination. The old sails being all used
up, his remains were placed in two meal-sacks and a weight
being fastened at foot, the body was placed upon one of
the hatch battens from which, when raised over the bul-
wark, it fell into the deep and was no more seen. He left
two little orphans, one of whom—a boy, seven years of
age—I noticed in the evening wearing his deceased father's

coat. Poor little fellow! He seemed quite unconscious of his loss and proud of the accession to his scanty covering. The remainder of the man's clothes were sold by auction by a friend of his who promised to take care of the children. There was great competition and the 'Cant', as they called it, occasioned jibing and jesting, which it was painful to listen to surrounded as were the actors (some of whom had just risen from a bed of sickness), by famine, pestilence and death.

Why America Appealed to Irish Immigrants

Arnold Schrier

In this article Arnold Schrier, the Walter C. Langsam Professor Emeritus of History at the University of Cincinnati, explains why many Irish immigrants found the idea of living in America appealing. The reasons the Irish came to America included the chance to participate in government, the opportunity to live in a democratic society, and most important for Irish immigrants, the chance to earn high wages. As Schrier shows through excerpts from letters from these immigrants to family members in Ireland, the newcomers were largely happy in their adopted country and encouraged relatives and friends to join them.

The image of America conjured up in Irish minds was the lure that beckoned young people westward across the Atlantic Ocean, an image made all the more attractive when contrasted with the unpromising picture of economic life in nineteenth-century Ireland. From countless bits and pieces of information was formed an alluring impression of America which came to predominate throughout the Irish countryside. Sometimes these tidbits of information were gleaned from travelers or "returned Yanks" or newspaper accounts, but for the vast majority of the population the greatest single source of knowledge was the myriad letters which flooded back from the emigrants in the New World. The American correspondent of the London *Daily*

Arnold Schrier, *Ireland and the American Emigration, 1850–1900*. Minneapolis: The University of Minnesota Press, 1958. Copyright © 1958 by The University of Minnesota Press, renewed 1985. Reproduced by permission.

News left no doubts on this point. Writing from New York in 1864, he was convinced that

> What brings such crowds to New York by every packet-ship is the letters which are written by the Irish already here to their relations in Ireland, accompanied, as they are in a majority of cases, by remittances to enable them to pay their passage out. It is from this source, and this mainly, if not only, that the Cork or Galway peasant learns all he knows about the United States, and he is not in the least likely to trust to any other.

Twelve years earlier a parish priest from County Armagh testified to the magnetic effect these letters had upon the people in his community, something he was well qualified to do since he read one third of all the American letters which came to his parish as a service for those who were illiterate. Even the newspapers of the period, while generally opposed to emigration, . . . could not help but mirror something of the attitude toward America which prevailed among the Irish. The "American fever" seemed to have permeated the entire country and no village, however small, was left unaffected. "It cannot be denied," observed the *Cork Examiner* in 1860, "that those feelings and motives [regarding America] have taken a deep root, and are very widely spread."

What was this image which made America so alluring? Part of the answer is to be found in the fact that Irish emigration to the United States was so widespread and of such a magnitude that by 1851 it was declared that America was no longer regarded as a foreign country, but as if Ireland were "part and parcel" of it. A little more than a decade later it was stated "as a matter of the driest fact" that there was "no country upon earth in whose well-being the Irish people have the same interest, as in that of the United States," and that it would be "impossible to touch the greatness, unity, or security of the United States, without wounding the interests of the Irish race [which are] inseparably connected with those of America." America, confessed one journal in 1873, had long been "the mainstay and the hope" of the Irish people, a hope, explained another, founded on the belief that in America they would "cultivate a soil without rent, earn plenty of money without being servants, and belong to a nation of sovereigns."

High Wages

The prospect of belonging to a nation of sovereigns seemed to some journals to be particularly appealing to the emigrants, for, unlike Ireland, America offered its citizens participation in the state so that its people felt they had a "stake in the country." But as it was true of the Irish who emigrated before the famine, so was it true of those who left in the fifty years following that catastrophe, that the chance to join a "ready-made Republic" was not nearly so important as was the promise of high wages. High wages, affirmed [Irish immigrant and Episcopalian bishop] William Forbes Adams, was America's one outstanding attraction for the Irish.

On this point most journals were in agreement. Even during the American Civil War it seemed natural, thought the *Northern Whig*, that Irishmen should prefer a land where there were "high wages for fair work." The journal also thought American society particularly well suited to the Irish because, "like all newly-organised societies, it is rude and boisterous." High wages, therefore, was the "bribe" held out to young emigrants and not, as some Tory newspapers insisted, the bounties offered for federal enlistment. Witnesses before parliamentary committees were also agreed that so long as people could not reap the benefits of their labors at home and so long as wages in America remained higher than they were in Ireland, just so long would young Irish men and women continue to be drawn from hearth and home. After all, it was pointed out, the Irish emigrant was not going to a wilderness but to join friends in a new home where hard work would procure for him a decent maintenance and a high degree of comfort. By the end of the century a legendary Irish bull had it that "The only place in Ireland where a man can make a fortune is in America."

No Idle Paradise

Newspapers of the period often attributed to the Irish peasant a vision of America as a land flowing with milk and honey, where the streets were paved with gold, and where all a body had to do to scoop up a fortune was to stoop down. If we may judge from the letters themselves, however, such romantic illusions were belied by the realism and general truthfulness which characterized the writers of these direct reports. America, they made clear, was no idle paradise. It was a hard-driving business country where rewards came only to those capable of hard work, thrift, and industriousness. The Yankees were a "go-ahead" people and to keep up with them one had to be like them. Consequently Irishmen worked harder and longer in America than they were ever inspired to do at home, and the phrase "hard work" runs like a constant refrain through practically all of the letters. But there were compensations. Strenuous labor was well rewarded with good wages, and while some immigrants pointed out that the high cost of living often reduced their real value, the prospect of high wages and constant employment became by far the two greatest attractions.

While the great majority of these immigrant scribes stressed the economic opportunities available in America, some also spoke of the social equality found here. This was a land that contained no titled nobility, where class divisions were fluid, and where an ascent of the economic lad-

der was usually accompanied by an ascent of the social ladder as well. The two themes, hard work and social equality, were well summed up by the *Galway Vindicator*,
which probably echoed the sentiments of a great many
Irishmen when it declared that America was a land where
"a man is a man if he's willing to toil." Occasionally some
writers reflected in their letters the tensions which developed between the Irish and the people who were pouring
into the country from other European nations, as between
the Irish and Scandinavians in the Midwest and the Irish
and Italians in the eastern cities. But for the most part
those who wrote home indicated that the Irish got along
well in America and that generally people had little difficulty in living with their neighbors.

Advice from Predecessors

A great many immigrants encouraged friends and relatives
to emigrate and in their letters often enclosed remittances
to help pay the cost of passage. Some also proffered sound
advice to the intending voyagers. America, they emphasized, was a country for young people, particularly unmarried ones, who were capable of long years of hard
work. Aware of an Irish inclination for imbibing immod-
erately, they often stressed the importance of temperate
habits and warned that drunkenness in America led only
to disgrace and degradation, advice which was seconded by
many newspapers. And like the newspapers, some writers
also urged those who intended to emigrate to avoid the
crowded eastern cities and travel to the interior or to the
Far West. A few advised young people to stay at home and
not emigrate at all if it were possible to live comfortably in
Ireland, but these seem to have been either older, less successful immigrants, or those who wrote during periods of
depression in America. . . .

Consciously or unconsciously the greater number of

those who wrote home seemed to be guided by the sensible advice of the Reverend John O'Hanlon, author of the most popular Irish-emigrant guidebook of the period. O'Hanlon cautioned the immigrants when writing home to remember that the "Utopia of the imagination is not the United States of our experience," and that by substituting "fancy for judgment, romantic hopes are first formed to be afterwards destroyed." Except in rare instances of deliberate misrepresentation, the immigrants appear to have had no wish to mislead their friends and family at home. Where overstatement did occur it was probably due much more to the first flush of enthusiasm attendant upon landing on American soil. This seems to have been the case with one young girl who landed in New York in 1850 and in her first letter home fairly gushed with praise:

> My dear Father I must only say that this is a good place and a good country for if one place does not suit a man he can go to another and can very easy please himself. . . . Any man or woman without a family are fools that would not venture and come to this plentyful Country where no man or woman ever hungered or ever will and where you will not be seen naked. . . .

If the greater number of letters were somewhat less exuberant in tone, their writers were no less definite in urging the Irish to try their fortunes in America. In 1854 a farm laborer in Illinois wrote to his friend in County Kildare that he was doing well enough so that by the following spring he hoped to own his farm and advised his friend to "come to this country and I know you will do well—one thing is certain you can be your own master a good deal sooner." He even offered to lend his friend money for passage and instructed him that he "need not be anyway shy in putting down a big figer. I would as soon send you £20 as one." Twenty-five years later a doctor in Iowa observed to his nephew in Ulster that "every man is his own landlord in this country—'Jack is as good as his Master.'" Some, as was the case with a railroad engineer in Cincinnati, were content to state simply that while they could never make a fortune in America, they could "earn an honest living."

Others were more forceful and one young emigrant working as a ranch hand near Puget Sound—at a time when the state of Washington was still a territory—not only offered to pay his brother's passage, but made clear to him why he thought it worthwhile to emigrate as soon as possible: "I still think I am in as good a country as there is in the world today for a poor man. The majority of what men is in the country have risen from their own industry. Any man here that will work and save his earnings, and make use of his brains can grow rich."

Only the Young Should Emigrate

America, however, was pre-eminently a place for young single people and this was something which many immigrants continually stressed. Old people were cautioned to stay away from a country where the pace of life and work would be too much for them. Such was the advice given by a young worker in Philadelphia in 1854 to his uncle, a farmer in Ulster:

> I have got along very well since I came here and has saved some money. I never regretted coming out here, and any young person that could not get along well there would do well to come here, if they intended to conduct themselves decently . . . but old people have no great chance here. . . .

From Iowa some fifteen years later an Irish farmer wrote to his brother in Dublin that "An unmarried man or girl can make out a living in any part of the country and have money too, provided he is not afraid of work," while a woman working as a domestic servant in Boston told her brother simply and directly in 1888 that "the younger they come the better." For young girls there was the added attraction of perhaps finding husbands who would not be so interested in their dowries, as was the custom in Ireland. One such colleen, who had broken off her courtship and left for Philadelphia, later wrote to her former beau that "Over in Ireland people marry for riches, but here in America we marry for love and work for riches.". . .

The Importance of Sobriety

If youth was stressed as a prerequisite for success, so was sobriety. Intemperance, it was asserted, was not only an evil in itself but a disgrace to an Irishman's birthland and his fellow countrymen. Americans, it was declared, detested drunkenness and the certain road to failure was via the bottle. Anyone who could not cure himself of the habit was better advised to stay home. A young lawyer who immigrated to Washington, D.C., in 1849 wrote to his uncle from that city four years later and told him that a good many Irish who were then living on the outskirts of the city were no models of ideal behavior:

> I am sorry to have it to say that by their fighting and drunkeness they are disgracing their country in the eyes of Americans. Generally speaking, *Americans dont drink [sic!]*, they are for the most part very temperate and disregard—detest the drunkard. Now instead of saving their wages, which are good, living orderly, keeping themselves and children clad, well, and clean, they are continually fighting among themselves: the Kerry men, and Clare men, and Limerick men: and for no other reason than this, because they were born in these different counties. But they have money to spend thus. So they have.

Over thirty years later a laborer in Boston told his family in County Cork that if his three brothers wished to emigrate he would try to help them,

> but I trust with the blessing of God none of them are fond of drink if they should be so it would be more ad-

visable to stop at home a Drunkered in America it would
be better for him to go to Mitchelstown poor house &
stope theire all his life. . . .

Hard Work

Youth and soberness were essential requirements for success in America, but even more fundamental was a capacity for hard work. Whether farm laborers or city workers,
whether in the eastern metropolises or the western ex-
panses, all were agreed that far more energy was expended
on the Atlantic's western side than was done on its eastern
shore. Unless one were prepared to put forth a great deal of
strenuous labor, it would be wiser to remain in Ireland. "Believe me," the young lawyer in Washington told his uncle in
1853, "there is no idle bread to be had here. If you get a
dollar a day, you have got to earn it *well*." Some thirty-five
years later a Boston laborer informed his family that "the
hard work of America is no joke, you must be able to hold
the cutting." In a letter the year before he advised that one
of his brothers get a job as a gardener before emigrating,
for that would "give him musle and make him firm & hard
which he or any other person must be for America.". . .

The Rewards of Immigration

The energy expended on American soil, however, usually
brought ample rewards, and unlike Ireland, where wages
were low and employment inconstant, in America there
was held out the promise of high wages and steady work.
Just how good the wages were was illustrated by the young
lawyer in Washington who told his uncle in 1853 that un-
questionably,

> This is a good country for a labouring man. . . . At this
> time he can earn at least one dollar a day, equal to 4
> shillings British. He is in good demand for this sum. He
> can board himself well—having meat three times a day,

for ten dollars a month—two dollars and a half a week,
or ten shillings British.

An agricultural laborer in Ireland in 1850, if he were fortunate enough in securing employment, received less than
five shillings a week for his labors, and rarely had meat
more than two or three times a year.

From Philadelphia in 1851 a young woman wrote to her
brother in Dublin that there was work for everyone and
"No female that can handle a needle need be idle." In San
Francisco that same year the prospects were even more alluring. In a letter published in the *Nation* it was claimed
that laborers in that city could earn from one to two
pounds per day. "If some of our hardy men of Tipperary
were here," exclaimed the writer, "what a fortune would be
open to them!". . .

Despite the caution that employment for men was
somewhat less constant than for women, the prospect of
earning thirty-six shillings a week must have seemed
tempting indeed to an Irish agricultural laborer whose
weekly wages in 1880 averaged no more than nine shillings
and in 1895 were still less than ten shillings. Little wonder
that with the impetus added by agrarian distress in Ireland
nearly three times as many people sailed for American
shores in 1880 as did the year before.

CHAPTER 2

Life in the United States for Famine Immigrants

COMING TO AMERICA

Living in the Tenements of New York City

Thomas Gallagher

Thomas Gallagher is the author of fiction and nonfiction works. In this selection from his book *Paddy's Lament: Ireland 1846–1847, Prelude to Hatred*, Gallagher uses fictional characters he calls Big Gil, Micky, and Dolores to show what typical Irish immigrants encountered as they tried to make their way through not only a new country but probably the largest and most confusing city most of them had ever seen, New York City. The immigrants found that the lodgings they could afford had passageways cluttered with rubbish, airless rooms, horses walking through hallways, unsafe staircases, and contaminated water supplies.

[As they] walked through the city, Big Gil and Micky asked Dolores to excuse them for a moment. They had noticed two privies in amongst some buildings in a backyard and, in the hope that no one would notice or mind, started through a passageway between two frame houses to where the privies stood. Next to the privies was another building, this one a six-story brick tenement, standing next to another of similar design in the center of what had been the adjacent backyards of the two one-family frame houses in front. This back area was surrounded by a picket fence, which also enclosed a number of pigsties and some stables.

The two tenements were separated by an airway about

Thomas Gallagher, *Paddy's Lament: Ireland 1846–1847, Prelude to Hatred*. New York: Harcourt Brace Jovanovich Publishers, 1982. Copyright © 1982 by Thomas Gallagher and Michael Gallagher. Reproduced by permission of the publisher.

twenty feet wide. The sun shone brightly, yet in this space, where thousands of worthless-looking rags and garments of every description hung from clotheslines, it was twilight. A fire-escape platform was attached to each of the windows, but none had a ladder leading to ground level, and every platform was choked anyway with boxes, coal scuttles, old tins, rags, and vegetables on their way to becoming garbage. On the ground, piled high against the picket fences, were rags mixed with bones, bottles, and papers, and straw and other substances so metamorphosed that the stench was almost unbearable. To make matters worse, the passageway between the two frame houses had become virtually impassable because of the filth created by the privies, pigs, and horses; to remedy this, planks had been laid. As Big Gil and Micky walked over these planks, a thick, brownish fluid oozed up like molasses through the spaces between them and completely covered the decaying boards that gave under their weight. The sight of the oozing fluid made even worse its smell, which reminded them of the steerage quarters they had just left.

The Sub-Landlord

No sooner did they start back from the privies to rejoin Dolores than they were caught by the sub-landlord.

"Wait, now, wait! Do you live here, or are you poaching? For as sure as I'm the landlord, the first is inside the law, the second outside."

Big Gil and Micky could see at once that the man confronting them was Irish; he had the red hair, blue eyes, and freckled cheeks to play Paddy [the nickname for the stereotypical Irishman] on any English stage. He was not as he claimed, the landlord, but rather the sub-landlord, carrying on for the real landlord, who had moved with his family uptown to Twenty-third Street.

"As for calling the police," Big Gil said in an effort to

placate the man, "it's equal to me whether you do or not. We're just off the ship *Mersey*, from Cork, looking as peacefully as anyone could wish for tenement accommodations." He had been hoping the man would have none to offer, but the man disappointed him.

"Accommodations, is it? Well, you've found them, then," the sub-landlord said, changing his tone and manner with the speed of a charlatan. "My name is John Maguire, I manage these premises, and I can assure you, your place is here, in the very heart of old New York, well situated and as airy as can be with the wind coming through the alleys off the water. Here, come with me. Let me show you an apartment I've been saving. At the very top of the stairs. Just under the roof. As full of air as a beach on Staten Island."

He was still Irish, but now separated from the old country by his knowledge of the Yankee's grasp of business, how it operated, and why it succeeded. Like so many others before him, he had arrived with that fatal Irish flaw: a willingness generated by a lifetime of oppression to do whatever was necessary to succeed in British-free America.

Big Gil and Micky had no choice but to pretend they were interested; they followed as Maguire, who also ran the saloon on the ground floor out front where Dolores was waiting, started through the tenement entrance into the hallway. Even Gil, a blacksmith long familiar with horses, was shocked to see that the only way the horses could enter or leave their stables in the yard was through the hallway of the tenement house, where the smell of manure permeated everything. John Maguire offered no explanation or apology for this as he led Big Gil and Micky up the stairs. If a pig could share the same hut with the family in Ireland, the horses could share the same tenement hallway with the tenants in New York.

The stairway was all rickety and out of level, with only

one or two of the balusters left on each flight to help keep the shaky handrail in place. Following the example of Maguire, who knew from experience how to steer clear of the dangers, they avoided the sagging middle of the stairs, worn from overuse to little more than a cardboard thickness. It was necessary to put your weight on either side of the stairs, where the upright board supporting each step offered the only secure footing.

"How do the tenants manage these stairs at night?" asked Big Gil.

"Ah, they do, going up or going down, with or without a drop in them, with no trouble worthy of mention."

He was not insulting their intelligence so much as assuming that they were used to such housing. Believing, as he obviously did, that the lodgings he had to offer in New York were no worse than those the Irish immigrants had left in Ireland, he spoke with the same equanimity as any landlord's agent would have in Ireland. Besides, he had the top-floor apartment to show them, and who in Ireland had ever lived six stories above the ground?

On the way up, they passed through hallways where the doors leading to the "apartments" were either ajar or wide open, giving every passer-by a view of the family living within. The families would of course have preferred privacy, but the doors had become so warped that they no longer fit the doorframes. The tenants would have had to shave either the edge of the door or the inside of the doorframe if they wanted privacy; none did, out of a fear instilled in them in Ireland that they would thus be destroying or altering someone else's property. What they did do, at night, was use rope to hold the doors as close to the doorframes as possible; during the day, with children coming and going, the rope proved to be more bother than help; the doors were allowed to remain open or ajar as their hinges dictated.

A Tenement Family

On the fourth floor, when Maguire, without so much as a "May I?," led Big Gil and Micky through one of these open doors to introduce them to the family living there, the family was no more surprised than he was apologetic. In a close, foul-smelling room measuring about twelve by fifteen feet, with nearly all the plaster off the walls, the fixtures stained yellow with smoke, and the wooden floor so greasy with refuse as to make it dangerous to walk on, they encountered a mother, married daughter, unemployed stepson, and four children—eight in all, counting the father, who was out laying water pipes in the street. Here they lived, cooked, and slept, four stories above the ground-level privies, which were so overused and in such bad order that the calls of nature were attended to in the room and the vessels carried downstairs to be emptied.

The stove, set in a corner by the window, was capable of accommodating but one pot at a time. Big Gil and Micky, fresh off the *Mersey*, were therefore not at all surprised to see a big steaming pot jammed with everything from scrap meat and bones down to potatoes, kidney beans, carrots, onions, peppercorns, soup greens of every variety, and a surface scum still to be scooped up and removed. The inviting smell emanating directly from the pot unfortunately combined with, rather than dispelled, all the other smells that had lodged themselves like permanent boarders in the apartment. You ate there, sitting at a table, only if you were awfully hungry; otherwise you stood by the stove, away from the other smells, with the steam of the food you were eating reminding you that it did indeed have a smell similar to the one you were tasting. The sub-landlord nevertheless continued to be proud—or at least not ashamed—of this property under his management as he led Big Gil and Micky to the "prize" he was offering them on the top floor.

Lack of Sanitation

These were the tenements awaiting the Irish in New York in 1847. Hurriedly built to accommodate the greatest number at the least expense, they had plumbing only on the ground level, where the crowding around spigots resembled the crowding around the ship's caboose on the way over. Not far from these spigots, on the same level, or in the basement, were the tenants' privies, overflowing with what was then euphemistically called "night soil." This noxious substance was carted away twice a week—if the tenants were lucky—by street department personnel, themselves Irish immigrants, who shoveled it into horse-drawn wagons and dumped it into the river on either side of the island before even the milkman was up to make his rounds.

It is true that people with dirty habits are likely to have dirty habitations and that a pauperized, intemperate people destroy the property they live in while making it the center of all kinds of vice and crime. But in 1847 it was a question not of which came first, the "dirty" Irish or the dirty tenements, but of how the tenements precluded any improvement in the way the Irish or any one else lived or wanted to live. The tenements not only led to dirty habits where none before existed; they choked off any nice habits the Irish might have brought with them or were likely to develop. To be dirty in these wretched, overcrowded tenements was easy; to be anything else was almost impossible.

Dedicated people like Dr. John H. Griscom, the city inspector of the Board of Health, found it shocking that most sub-landlords were once immigrants themselves. He and his staff were baffled that men who had started up the social ladder were the first to knock down, if they could, those just below them. These Irish sub-landlords were among the hardest bargainers, the most unprincipled cheats, to confront the newly arrived immigrant. By running the groggeries [saloons] and groceries attached to the tenements from which they collected rents, they were able to keep a daily check on their tenants while pressing vice and other evils on them. The sub-landlords knew their bars would be well attended by tenants happy that their drinking companions were also Catholic. In such an establishment, dismal and cellar-damp though it might be, there would be no reason to mince matters with those of other religious persuasions or, worse, to disguise one's religious beliefs for fear of being unpopular. Rare was the Irishman who would do such a thing; indeed, whenever two or three Irishmen entered a tavern frequented by Protestant nativists, it did not take long for a violent brawl to erupt and spread into the street.

Had the Irish been members of one of the Protestant sects whose churches dotted the streets of New York, their brogue, their poverty, even their crazy hats and coats, would have been looked upon as quaint rather than disgusting; they would have been accepted and helped, ushered through the inevitable acculturation process. But their religion confirmed and perpetuated the stigma that their Gaelic language, brogue, and poverty made so obvious. Anyone wearing one of those decrepit swallow-tailed coats and ridiculously battered high hats was not simply another immigrant; he was another Irish Catholic immigrant.

The Wealthy Slumlords

In New York, this tenement-groggery arrangement developed from a pattern established long before the arrival of the famine Irish. The wealthy had built townhouses in all the nooks and corners of Manhattan's toe, on property owned by them, at a time when the vest-pocket size of New York made living there charming as well as convenient for both family life and business. The head of the family walked, rode a horse, or was taken in a carriage to his office, law firm, court building, or hospital, while his wife took the children to and from a nearby private school, shopped for clothes at Steward's on Broadway, visited friends, attended teas, and supervised the cook and maids at home.

But as the population grew and the incoming ships unloaded more and more merchandise from all over the world, this entire lower part of the island became dominated by business. Shops, fabric stores, oyster bars, and barrooms proliferated in every street; factories, tanneries, slaughterhouses, hotels, and tenements cropped up all over, until wealthy property owners began to leave their townhouses for the more respectable and less crowded areas stretching as far north as Forty-second Street.

The wealthy knew better than to sell this valuable downtown property; they engaged, instead, sub-landlords to superintend it for them. The almost immediate result, given the low cost of labor and materials at the time, was the erection of six-story tenements where none had before existed—in the very backyards of the townhouses vacated by the wealthy. Now, instead of flower and vegetable gardens back to back, there were two six-story tenements facing each other, the distance between them so close that immigrants reaching out from one could, in some cases, touch fingers with those reaching out from the other.

The original townhouses remained and were themselves occupied from cellar to attic, the cellar by tenants or perhaps by an oyster bar, the next floor by the owner of the oyster bar, who was usually the sub-landlord as well, and all the floors above, into the highest attic recesses, by desperate and exhausted immigrants who had decided, in most cases correctly, that they had no other choice.

The Cellar Dwellers

Meanwhile, Dolores, still waiting for her friends out front, had become aware of the squinting windows on either side of the street, where the façades of these townhouses faced each other. She was being watched by already-settled Irish immigrants, just as she might have been back home in a city's Irish town, where the Catholic poor lived separate and apart from the Protestant well-to-do. When the Protestants rode through these Irish towns on horseback or in carriages, they were watched with hatred and envy from behind broken, half-boarded windows that look like eyes damaged in drunken brawls. But this was New York, Dolores was obviously another Irish Catholic immigrant, and behind the windows now were mothers and grandmothers who should have remained in Ireland and died there rather than here. Too old to be left alone in Ireland and too weak to refuse passage, they had left and were now peering out in the hope that Dolores's appearance would add something extra to this particular day in their lives. Through what seemed a dim mist of time, they watched her standing there, the whites of their eyes, the cheekbones of their gaunt faces, and the tight knuckles of their hands flashing through the dark windows like flecks of dying hope.

When Big Gil and Micky rejoined her, she said in passing that she had seen several Irish women and children coming up from the cellars of the frame houses fronting on the street.

Big Gil nodded: "The 'cellar population,' the mate on the *Mersey* called them. They're even poorer, he said, than the tenement population in the rear."

"I've had my turn in the rear," Micky said. "And if ever it comes to that, I'll take the cellar over the tenement."

New York's Filthy Streets

It was said that the steady influx of Irish immigrants from rural environment made sanitary laws unenforceable, but the streets of New York had always been used as a depository for garbage, rubbish, and offal. Wealthy New Yorkers had for years hired help to keep the streets clean in front of their townhouses. Some who could not afford this service refused to be seen sweeping side by side with the servants of their wealthy neighbors. The result was that even in the better neighborhoods, and long before the influx of the famine Irish, pedestrians had to be careful where they walked.

Mayhem and Muck

In the busier streets, the hawking of fish, vegetables, and joints of beef and pork added to the problem, since peddlers used the gutters as receptacles for fish heads, the viscera and trimmings of butchered animals, and the unedible husks, leaves, and greens from cauliflower, carrots, corn, beets, and lettuce. The ever-roaming swine of New York induced these peddlers to toss their refuse in the streets, and this in turn encouraged the Irish poor to acquire more pigs and piglets to roam the streets for food at no one's expense. Even when the piles of garbage, rubbish, dirt, blood, dead animals, and store and shop sweepings were removed in response to citizens' complaints, the offal wagon would no sooner turn the corner than the accumulation of decaying vegetable and animal matter would begin again, once more to be examined by the accommodating pigs.

Some streets in the tenement districts looked more like dunghills than thoroughfares in a civilized city. The gutters were loaded with, the sewer culverts obstructed by, everything from house slops to human excrement, the latter carried down in buckets from the tenements and emptied in the street because the night-soil man had failed to come by and empty the overflowing backyard privies. At irregular intervals, street cleaners with tarpaulin-covered carts would come round and rake out the black and decayed contents of these deep gutters on either side of the street. Nothing on earth smelled worse, especially during the summer months when the amount of waste matter increased along with the temperature needed to accelerate its decomposition. During interims when the street cleaner failed to appear for a week or more, the putrifying organic substances were ground together by the constantly passing horses and vehicles into a poisonous powder, clouds of which were raised by the endless traffic and carried by the wind in every direction.

These nuisances alone would have been enough to tax the patience of visitors to the city, let alone of those living, working, and doing business every day within its limits. But the city's manure problem far exceeded even that of the garbage and offal. In 1847 there were in the city over six thousand public and private stables, accommodating over sixty thousand horses. The average manure production per horse per month being 0.43 tons, New York's total production per annum was well over 309,000 tons, almost all of it confined to the tightly packed area between The Battery and Canal Street. . . .

Staying in the City

Commentators during these years advised Irishmen to get out of New York and go west, north, or south to rural America where they belonged. But the Irish had seen their fathers and grandfathers in the old country work the land from youth to old age with nothing to show for it but a bent back. They were disenchanted with farming, and they liked the clannishness of the Irish in New York, the political corruption they perceived in the city, the easy access—not once but several times—to the polling booth. They all had witnessed the court system in Ireland, which the French writer Gustave de Beaumont had called "a lie of forms . . . a preparation for vengeance." Now the same kind of deceit, deception, and dishonesty might be theirs to channel through Tammany Hall[1] for their own benefit.

Besides, the great city they had in so many ways feared turned out to be not so foreign and unaccommodating after all. The horses and pigs in the streets, the slaughterhouses and tanneries, the stables and blacksmiths' shops and all the rural smells they created, the hotels with their efficient Irish servant girls and slender young Irish waiters, the burly Irishmen laying the city's gas lines and Croton Water Works pipes in the streets—all these made staying in New York City more attractive than heading into the unknown countryside, where building canals, cutting through forests, laying railroad lines, or working the land presented almost the only ways to exist, all of them in lonely places bereft of the kind of "society" most Irishmen craved.

Hatred for England

Then too, living in New York City, with the ocean beside them, made Ireland and their loved ones nearer, and what England had done to them easier to remember. This abiding hatred of the British delayed what would otherwise have been a speedy acculturation. The entrenched New Yorkers were, after all, of British or Dutch descent, and despite the Revolutionary War, British culture had no more been discarded by the wealthy than it was when King's College was renamed Columbia. Even the Gaelic-speaking Irish eventually acquired their inimitable version of the English tongue and were able to use it with the same dexterity that they had heard it used, minus the brogue and at their expense, in Ireland's courtrooms. Still, they became "American" very fast—except for their Catholicism, their distrust and misuse of government, and the alacrity with which they expressed, anywhere and in front

1. the headquarters of the Irish American political "machine"

of anybody, their hatred of the British Empire. Having lived so long with this cancer of hidden resentment, they could not wait in New York to expose it to anyone who would or could be forced to listen.

Nor did the Irish in the Midwest, surrounded by land whose fertility exceeded the wildest stories they had heard in Ireland, lose this hatred; they simply became too busy with and rooted in their new land to cling so tenaciously to the horrors and causes of the famine. They would go on being as faithful to Ireland and their loved ones as the easterners, but they would at the same time become more engulfed in America, in the entire continent surrounding them, in the work they had to put in on what they could at last call their own land, with no religious tithes attached and no pig needed for the absentee landlord's rent.

The Anti-Catholic Climate in Nineteenth-Century America

Charles R. Morris

In this article writer Charles R. Morris describes the attitude of many Americans in the nineteenth century toward the Catholic Church and Catholic immigrants. To illustrate the near hysteria that was building in some parts of the United States toward the influx of Catholics, the majority of whom were Irish immigrants, he begins by relating how a mob attacked and set fire to the Catholic Ursuline Convent in Charlestown, Massachusetts. After detailing how the convent was attacked and burned, Morris describes the ensuing wave of anti-nun literature and the formation of the Know-Nothing political party, which held anti-Catholic views.

The [Catholic Ursuline Convent in Charlestown, Massachusetts] burst into unwonted prominence in the late spring of 1834 when a young townswoman, Rebecca Reed, claimed that after converting to Catholicism and becoming a nun, she had "escaped" from the Ursuline Convent. Her account of the adventure was made into a book, *Six Months in a Convent*, that was widely circulated in Charlestown and Boston. (It is a dull affair, obviously written by a Puritan divine, and full of elaborate ceremonials with wax tapers that would shock only a fundamentalist minister.) Sr. Edmond met the charges with disdain—Reed had been a convent serving girl discharged for dishonesty—but she intensified her calling schedule on Charlestown's leading families.

In late July, a real nun made a real escape. Edward Cutter, who owned a brickyard next to the convent, was astonished one night to open his door to a young woman with close-cropped hair and wild eyes, dressed only in a nightshift, begging to be taken to her brother in Boston. The poor woman was Elizabeth Harrison, who had suffered a nervous breakdown and had been confined to the convent infirmary. At her brother's house the next day, she changed her mind and agreed to return to the convent. Once the story was broadcast that she was back in the convent, however, rumors quickly spread that she had been dragged kicking and screaming from her brother's house, and was being confined in a "deep dungeon."

Reactions to the Rumors

As the Boston and Charlestown papers trumpeted the case of the kidnapped nun, fiery meetings were held in Charlestown. The ringleaders were apparently Cutter, Alvah Kelley, the owner of another nearby brickyard, and the area's Congregationalist ministers. Storming the convent was on the agenda from the very start; one meeting resolved to "leave not one stone unturned of that curst Nunnery that prostitutes female virtue and liberty under the garb of holy religion." On Sunday, August 10, Lyman Beecher, the father of Harriet Beecher Stowe [author of *Uncle Tom's Cabin*] and a leading Congregationalist minister, delivered a blistering harangue, "The Devil and the Pope of Rome," to a large audience, pointedly denouncing the Ursulines. A number of other Congregationalist ministers delivered violent sermons on the same day. Court records strongly imply that the ministers knew that an attack on the convent was planned for the next night and were purposely whipping up tempers.

On Monday, Charlestown's selectmen, who clearly also knew of the planned attack, made a last-ditch call on Sr. Edmond, and she reluctantly agreed to admit Cutter, whom she considered a friend. Cutter met with Harrison, who was by now calm and self-possessed, and clearly not being held against her will, and made enough of a tour to confirm there was no dungeon. He, Kelley, and the selectmen wrote a statement for the next day's papers exonerating the convent. Cutter and Kelley apparently worked the rest of the day to head off the attack, but events had already passed beyond their control.

Mobs gathered in front of the convent on Monday night, demanding the release of the imprisoned nun. Sr. Edmond, who must have been a formidable woman, met them at the gate, and sent one mob off. When a larger crowd arrived and lit bonfires, she once again went out and stunned them into silence, and for a moment at least, had them in her hand. Then she overstepped: "Disperse immediately," she said, "for if you don't, the Bishop has twenty thousand Irishmen at his command in Boston and they will whip you all into the sea." The crowd responded with an outraged roar, someone fired a musket at the nun, and she beat a retreat to the convent as the mob assaulted the gate. The nuns and girls escaped into the garden—Elizabeth Harrison was in hysterics, blaming herself for the attack—and an older nun who was ill did not survive the night. The mob stormed through the gate and charged the convent, rampaging from room to room, smashing furniture and china, and setting the rooms on fire. Drunken rowdies put on nuns' habits and danced lewdly around bonfires of books and furniture. The fire company arrived but did not intervene, because they were either complicit or frightened.

When the fire forced the mob to retreat from the buildings, platoons of armed men with torches began searching the grounds for the nuns and the girls, who were trapped in the garden against the iron fence. On the verge of panic, they were saved by Cutter and workers from his brickyard, who cut through the fence and spirited them away to Cutter's house. The mob spread through Charlestown, and a number of Irish homes were attacked and burned. Cutter had to move the girls twice more during the night as bands of men pressed their search. The bloody mood finally dissipated with the dawn. The rioters, by then exhausted and happy, many of them still in nuns' habits, twirling rosaries and singing hymns, streamed back across the bridge to Boston, as the convent smoldered up on the hill. The girls, who had been hiding nearby, and anxious to get back to their families, joined in the procession, most of them still in their nightclothes. . . . An eventual trial acquitted everyone but a young boy, who was pardoned because of his age.

Anti-Nun Literature

The burning of the convent unleashed a great sordid wave of anti-nun literature, including at least three novelistic treatments of the Ursuline Convent, all of it full of a crawly, peek-through-the-curtain prurience—lubricious tales of satanic rituals behind the granite walls, of nuns as sex slaves, as baby murderers, as torturers, with hints of darker perversions that could not be spoken. The tales follow a consistent pattern: An innocent young girl, full of love for Christ, decides to enter a convent to dedicate her life to God. Her first days at the convent and her novitiate proceed as expected. She is dutiful and prayerful, although her superiors seem stern and cold. But there are mysterious doors she may not enter, ceremonies she may not attend, unexplained footfalls in the night, until finally she becomes a nun and the full horrors of the cloister are revealed.

The paradigmatic nun's tale was Maria Monk's *Awful*

Disclosures. Published in 1836, it sold at least 300,000 copies before the Civil War, and probably twice that by the end of the century, for there were many pirate versions. It has been called the *Uncle Tom's Cabin* of anti-Catholicism, or the anti-Catholic equivalent of the anti-Semitic *Protocols of the Elders of Zion.* Maria Monk claimed to have received the veil after a normal preparatory period at the Hôtel Dieu convent in Montreal. On the night of her induction, to her great shock, she discovered that her primary religious duty, as for the other young nuns, was to slake the lusts of monks and priests who came scuttling each night through a tunnel from a nearby monastery. Numerous babies, of course, were born in the convent, and the older nuns made a ceremony of baptizing and then smothering them, to ensure that they "were at once admitted into heaven," tossing the little corpses into a lime pit in the basement. Maria saw three babies murdered, and was forced to participate in the trial and execution of a nun who had protested against the murder of her baby. When the bishop pronounced the death sentence, the victim was tied to a mattress, another mattress was piled on top, and a whole crowd of nuns and priests jumped up and down on her until she died.

The actual provenance of Maria Monk's tale was established within a relatively short time of publication. Maria, her mother confirmed, had been an unmanageable child who spent a brief time in a Catholic orphanage in Montreal, although she was not herself Catholic. She had certainly never been a nun, or ever inside the Hôtel Dieu. Maria became pregnant in Montreal and was brought to New York by William Hoyt, a former priest and a leader of the Canadian anti-Catholic movement. (According to Maria's mother, he was also the father of her child.) Hoyt introduced her to a group of nativists in New York, including several leading ministers, who financed her confinement and concocted the story. Besides the ministers, the group included Theodore Dwight, a grandson of [well-known eighteenth-century minister] Jonathan Edwards, a brother of the late president of Yale, and editor of the nativist *Hartford Courant*.

The Rev. J.J. Slocum, one of the group, later admitted drafting most of the manuscript, but with the close participation of the others. Slocum insisted that he wrote only at Maria's dictation, although a number of scenes—the lecheries, the prisoners in the basement, sexual abuse during confession—track closely with the staple anti-Catholic screeds that the ministers knew so well. Nor were the ministers deluded as to Maria's character; while they were composing a follow-up volume, she took off from New York to be with a lover in Philadelphia. They claimed she had been kidnapped by a band of priests.

Compounding the disgrace, the ministers were as motivated by money as by religious bile. When the manuscript was finished, it was taken to the publisher James Harper, a friend of Dwight and later a nativist mayor of New York. Harper formed a shell company to distribute the book, since he thought it too racy for his own imprint. Advance publicity included installments of the book's juiciest episodes in a nativist journal, *The American Protestant Vindicator*, and sold-out lectures for Maria. The financial arrangements were disclosed in two separate court actions, in 1836 and 1837, in which Slocum and Maria sued unsuccessfully for their profits. The copyright, and apparently all the profits, accrued to Harper, Hoyt, and one other of the ministers. Poor Maria seems to have gotten nothing at all.

By the time of the court actions, discriminating Protestants were already embarrassed by their initial credulous acceptance of *Awful Disclosures*. The New York publisher William Stone, a fair-minded nativist, called at the convent while in Montreal on business, and persuaded the nuns to permit him to examine the premises. He toured with Maria's book in hand and confirmed that none of its physical descriptions of the convent, which were quite detailed and included a complete floor plan, bore any resemblance to the actual place; nor did a minute inspection of the basements disclose a tunnel to a monastery or a lime pit for infant corpses. Stone wrote a full report that concluded: "I most solemnly believe that the nuns and priests are innocent in this matter"—touching off a baroque intra-Protestant controversy, highlighted by the publication of a mock-epic poem satirizing his visit, which was answered by a full-length play.

The discrediting of Maria had little effect on book sales, which continued strong for decades. The anti-Catholic magazines that had first publicized the story, like the *Vindicator* and *The Downfall of Babylon*, became overnight successes, spawning imitators throughout the country. The low point may have been the publication of *Dreadful Scenes in the Awful Disclosures*, a hot-selling folio of "artists' conceptions" of the lurid doings at the Hôtel Dieu. None of it benefited Maria. She was cast aside by her handlers and bore another child out of wedlock in 1838, making no pretense that it had been fathered by a priest. She had a brief failed marriage, became an alcoholic, was arrested for picking pockets in a New York bordello, and died in prison in 1849.

Violence Against Catholics

The burning of the Ursuline Convent was the first salvo in two decades of violence against immigrants and Catholics, to the drum music of unceasing, often wildly paranoid diatribes against the scandals and corruptions in the Roman Church. For at least a year after the burning of the convent, Catholics in Boston and Charlestown had to post armed guards around their churches, and Bishop Fenwick was shot in effigy in 1835. A mob burned down most of Boston's Irish quarter in 1837, and another mob attacked an Irish-American militia company. Letters in the All Hallows archives testify to church burnings throughout the country during the 1840s. Irish and native mobs clashed repeatedly in New York, Philadelphia, and Detroit, and pitched battles were a feature of almost every big-city election day. German Catholics were attacked in St. Louis, and later themselves attacked nativist speakers, while German and nativist mobs fought in Louisville and Cincinnati. The Irish, in particular, often gave as good as they got. Irish mobs beat up Protestants in upstate New York and attacked blacks in Philadelphia, and German and Irish workers fought constantly on the railroads. In 1841, in the face of repeated nativist threats [bishop of New York] John Hughes made his famous statement that he would turn New York into "a second Moscow" if nativists attacked his churches, and for a long time armed Irishmen did nightly guard duty outside New York's Catholic institutions.

The curve of tension came to a head in Philadelphia in 1844, in what one scholar has described as nothing less than "a brutal ethnoreligious war." Philadelphia had boomed in the 1830s and had the largest concentration of Irish Catholic immigrants outside of New York. The event that precipitated the violence was specifically religious. Francis Kenrick, Philadelphia's archbishop, had quietly negotiated a series of concessions to alleviate Catholic discomfort with Protestant Bible-reading in public schools—a divisive issue in almost every big eastern city. But a garbled story spread through nativist circles that an Irish politician and school board member, Hugh Clark, had forcibly interfered with a Bible lesson in a local school. It soon became clear that Clark had behaved properly, but the local nativist party, the American Republicans, held a protest meeting anyway, and Irish hecklers disrupted the meeting.

In retaliation, the nativists, led by a pugnacious Jew named Lewis Levin, turned out some 3000 people on Monday, May 6, for an anti-Catholic rally in Kensington, just north of the city proper, and the heart of Philadelphia's Irishtown. Fighting broke out when a sudden rainstorm sent the crowd fleeing for the Nanny Goat Market, a roofed open-air bazaar that was clearly Irish territory. A nativist youth fired a pistol, striking an Irish bystander in the face. The Irish pulled their own weapons, but were quickly routed in a hail of bricks and paving stones. Irish musketmen then opened fire on the market from the surrounding houses. Gun battles raged for the next three days, with fatalities on both sides, as nativists mounted repeated assaults on Kensington. The confrontation ended only after the nativists burned out most of the area, killing a number of the Irish and chasing the rest to the woods north of the city, where at least one woman died from exposure. After burning down St. Michael's Church, the mob marched into downtown Philadelphia and burned St. Augustine's Church at Fourth and Vine, near the entrance to the present-day Benjamin Franklin Bridge. The mayor confronted the mob on the steps of St. Augustine's, but a hail of stones sent him scurrying for his life.

A few weeks later, a second round of rioting broke out on the south side of the city, when nativists attacked a church that contained a store of Irish weapons. The militia intervened, and a wild melee ensued, with upper-class cavalry officers, who were perfectly ecumenical in their disdain for the lower classes, charging up and down the dark streets stabbing and shooting at nativists. The nativists strung ropes to trip the troopers' horses and fired barrages of scrap iron from two small cannons stolen from the shipyard. When it was over, thirteen people were dead, including two soldiers, and the number of wounded ran into the scores. . . .

The Know-Nothing Party

This was the atmosphere in which the national Know-Nothing party, or the Order of the Star-Spangled Banner, was officially organized in the summer of 1854, on a platform of straightforward nativism and anti-Catholicism, and with the full panoply of secret handshakes, finger signs, codes, alarm signals, costumes, and funny hats that nineteenth-century clubmen so loved. Even before their national convention, Know-Nothings had captured the mayoralty of Philadelphia. In November, they won 63 percent of the vote in Massachusetts, taking every state senate seat and all but two assembly seats, and they took 40 percent of the ballots in Pennsylvania and 25 percent in New York. The following year, the Know-Nothings swept local elections throughout New England and made major inroads in California and the South. One hundred and twenty-one congressmen counted themselves among the Know-Nothings in 1854. When the party nominated former president Millard Fillmore as their candidate for the 1856 election, experienced observers expected the Know-Nothings to inherit the Whig mantle. One leading historian has argued that it was only a north-south split within the Know-Nothings that prevented nativism, rather than antislavery, from becoming the organizing principle of the emerging new Republican Party. . . .

The Irish Immigrants

America . . . was already slipping its psychological moorings just as it was hit by the great wave of Famine-inspired Irish immigration. The economy was veering between extremes of inflation and depression, revolutions in Europe were disrupting trade, the war with Mexico was wildly unpopular. Henry David Thoreau meditated publicly on civil disobedience, and the sectional divisions that foreshadowed the Civil War dominated national politics. A rural nation found itself confronting runaway urban growth. New York City's population quadrupled in the thirty years to 1860; Chicago's grew even faster. In 1820, there were only twelve cities with more than 10,000 people; in 1860, there were 101 such cities and eight with more than 100,000. One out of every five Americans lived in a city by 1860, up from only 6 percent in 1820.

The feeling of a world awry easily slipped into a racist reaction against the new immigrants. Here is the New York City diarist George Templeton Strong in 1848 (he was building a house): "Hibernia [Ireland] came to the rescue yesterday morning; twenty 'sons of toil' with prehensile paws supplied them by nature with evident reference to the handling of the spade and the wielding of the pickaxe and congenital hollows on the shoulder wonderfully adapted to make the carrying of the hod a luxury instead of a labor." Charles O'Conor—whom Strong detested while grudgingly admitting his abilities—was still working his way up the ladder of the New York bar when he lamented, "This is an English colony [with] the true Saxon contempt for everything Irish."

To be fair to the nativists, the Irish imposed immense public costs. More than 80 percent of the Irish settled in cities, so by themselves they accounted for a sizable fraction of the urbanizing trend and for much of the frightening growth in the armies of unemployed laborers. The severe shortfalls in sewage, water supply, police, and sanitary services that plagued midcentury cities could, without bigotry, be traced directly to the Irish. Poor-relief expenditures in Boston quadrupled between 1840 and 1860. The Irish accounted for three-quarters of Boston's arrestees and police detainees by the 1860s, and 55 percent of New York's. Irish pigs running loose in lower Manhattan were the despair of New York health authorities, and former mayor Philip Hone remarked that "Bishop Hughes deserves a cardinal's hat at least for what he has done in placing Irish Catholics on the necks of native New Yorkers." An *Atlantic Monthly* columnist lamented, almost with disbelief, that just a few decades before Boston could brag of but "little poverty, little gross ignorance, and little crime." Even Irish apologists like Thomas D'Arcy McGee admitted that the Irish needed time and understanding to learn the habits and disciplines required in their new country. Old-line Americans, already under siege by the Henry Halfacres[1] of the world, found the success of Irish-based political machines especially galling—Irishmen "fresh from the bogs . . . led up to vote like dumb brutes." Anger against the Irish naturally translated into anti-Catholicism.

1. a character created by the writer James Fenimore Cooper

A Continuous Struggle: Irish Workers in Mid-Nineteenth-Century America

Ronald Takaki

Ronald Takaki teaches in the ethnic studies department at the University of California at Berkeley and has written several books about the immigrant experience in America and the contributions of immigrants to American society. In this selection Takaki describes the kinds of work Irish immigrants usually did in the middle of the nineteenth century, such as building roads, railroads, and canals and working in factories. He also relates how in their struggle to find work, Irish immigrants found themselves pitted against African Americans and Chinese immigrants. According to Takaki, animosity often arose among these ethnic groups as they struggled to find their place in a society that looked down upon certain immigrants.

Irish immigrants provided the labor for the construction or roads and canals for the Market Revolution. Watching them work on the National Road in Pennsylvania, a farmer described them as an "immortal Irish brigade, a thousand strong, with their carts, wheelbarrows, shovels and blasting tools, grading the commons, and climbing the mountainside . . . leaving behind them a roadway good enough

Ronald Takaki, *A Different Mirror: A History of Multicultural America*. New York: Little, Brown and Company, 1993.

for an emperor to travel over." Irish laborers helped to build waterways, including Connecticut's Enfield Canal, Rhode Island's Blackstone Canal, and, most important, New York's Erie Canal, described by Reverend Buckley as "one of the grandest pieces of engineering ever seen in the world" and "proof" of "Irish talent.". . .

Irish workers built thousands of miles of rail lines such as the Western and Atlantic Railroad from Atlanta to Chattanooga and the Union Pacific segment of the transcontinental railroad. All day they were ordered: "Now Mick do this, and Mick do that." And they shouted back: "The devil take the railroad!". . .

The pervasive presence of the Irish in railroad work produced the popular saying that there was "an Irishman buried under every tie." Indeed the Irish had high accident rates, for they were frequently assigned the hazardous jobs. A Connecticut ax manufacturer explained that he employed the Irish as grinders because the death rate due to accidents was so high he had difficulty finding "Yankees" to do this dangerous work. "My father carried the mark of the quarry to his grave," wrote [political activist] Elizabeth Gurley Flynn. "When he was a boy, working in a quarry in Maine, carrying tools, the sight of one eye was destroyed by a flying chip of granite.". . .

Irish laborers, an immigrant complained, were "thought nothing of more than *dogs* . . . despised & kicked about." They lived in "clumsy, rough and wretched hovels," made with "roofs of sod and grass" and "walls of mud," observed [English writer] Charles Dickens during a visit to the United States. "Hideously ugly old women and very buxom young ones, pigs, dogs, men, children, babies, pots, kettles, dung hills, vile refuse, rank straw and standing water, all wallowing together in an inseparable heap, composed the furniture of every dark and dirty hut." America turned out to be a nightmare for many Irish immigrants.

They had crossed the ocean in pursuit of riches, but they failed to find "gold on the street corner."

The Irish Pitted Against Other Workers

Instead, Irish immigrants found themselves not only exploited as laborers but also pitted against workers of other races, including the Chinese. While competition between Irish and Chinese workers was extensive in California, it dramatically surfaced in New England. Workers in the shoemaking industry were struggling against low wages and the introduction of labor-eliminating machines; consequently, they organized the Secret Order of the Knights of St. Crispin. The Crispins quickly became the largest labor organization in the United States; in 1870, it had a membership of 50,000. Demanding higher wages and an eight-hour day, the Crispins went out on strike at a shoe factory in North Adams, Massachusetts. The owner, Calvin T. Sampson, fired the disgruntled workers and pursued a strategy of divide-and-control by driving a "wedge" between himself and the strikers.

This "wedge" turned out to be a contingent of seventy-five Chinese workers from San Francisco. Brought to North Adams as scabs to break the Irish strike, they were housed in dormitories inside the locked and guarded gates of the factory yard. Sampson's experiment caught the attention of other capitalists as well as the national news media. Within three months after their arrival in North Adams, the Chinese workers were producing more shoes than the same number of white workers had been making before the strike. The success of Sampson's strategy was celebrated in the press. "The Chinese, and this especially annoys the Crispins," the editor of *The Nation* wrote, "show the usual quickness of their race in learning the process of their new business, and already do creditable hand and machine work."

The Chinese were held up as a model for Irish laborers. Writing for *Scribner's Monthly*, William Shanks compared the Chinese to the Irish workers. The Chinese "labored regularly and constantly, losing no blue Mondays[1] on account of Sunday's dissipations nor wasting hours on idle holidays," he reported. "The quality of the work was found to be fully equal to that of the Crispins." Through the use of Chinese labor, Sampson had widened his profit margin: the weekly saving in labor costs was $840, or $40,000 a year. These figures inspired Shanks to calculate: "There are 115 establishments in the State, employing 5,415 men . . . capable of producing 7,942 cases of shoes per week. Under the Chinese system of Mr. Sampson, a saving of $69,594 per week, or say $3,500,000 a year, would be effected, thus revolutionizing the trade."

In their response to Sampson's "wedge," the Irish strikers tried to promote working solidarity by trying to organize a Chinese lodge of St. Crispin. Watching this initiative to build Irish-Chinese unity, the editor of *The Nation* commented: "Chinese lodges and strikes will come in time when enough Chinamen are collected together in any given place; but the prospect appears not immediately flattering at North Adams." Based on self-interest rather than an ideological commitment to class solidarity this attempt to unionize the Chinese workers quickly collapsed. At a meeting in Boston, white workers turned against the Chinese laborers, condemning them for reducing "American labor" to "the Chinese standard of rice and rats."

Sampson's daring action had a sobering effect on striking workers at nearby shoe factories. Ten days after the arrival of Sampson's "Mongolian battery," Parker Brothers, Cady Brothers, Millard and Whitman, and E.R. and N.L. Millard were able to force their laborers to return to work

1. referring to workers calling in sick with hangovers on Mondays

with a 10 percent wage cut. Commenting on the signifi-
cance of Sampson's experiment of substituting Chinese
for Irish laborers, a writer for *Scribner's Monthly* observed: "If for no other purpose than the breaking up of
the incipient steps toward labor combinations and Trade
Unions . . . the advent of Chinese, labor should be hailed
with warm welcome." The "heathen Chinee," he concluded, could be the "final solution" to the labor problem
in America.

Being Compared to Blacks

While they were contrasted with the Chinese, Irish immigrants found themselves compared to blacks. During the
mid–nineteenth century, anti-Irish stereotypes emphasized
nature over nurture and descent over consent. The Irish
were imaged as apelike and "a race of savages," at the same
level of intelligence as blacks. Pursuing the "lower" rather
than the "higher" pleasures, seeking "vicious excitement"
and "gratification merely animal," the Irish were said to
be "slaves" of "passion." Since sexual restraint was the
most widely used method of birth control, the large families of these immigrants seemed to indicate a lack of self-
control: "Did wealth consist in children, it is well known
that the Irish would be rich people. . . ." In a sermon on
"The Dangerous Classes," Reverend Theodore Parker of
Boston identified the "inferior peoples in the world,"
claiming that some were "inferior in nature, some perhaps
only behind us in development" on "a lower form in the
great school of Providence—negroes, Indians, Mexicans,
Irish, and the like.". . .

Like blacks, Irish workers were condemned for lacking
the habits of punctuality and industry. They were dismissed from their jobs for laziness, gambling, drinking,
and "other debaucheries," as well as for "levity" and "im-
pudence." A saying claimed: "It's as natural for a Hibern-

ian to tipple as it is for a pig to grunt." Their "idleness"
and "brutal leprosy of blue Monday habits," it was argued,
rendered them unreliable as workers and kept them impoverished. Like the "giddy multitude" of seventeenth-
century Virginia, the Irish were chastised as an unruly and
disorderly laboring class. In Jersey City, Irish workers were
denounced by a newspaper editor as "a mongrel mass of
ignorance and crime and superstition, as utterly unfit for
its duties, as they [were] for the common courtesies and
decencies of civilized life." Irish children, moreover, were
seen as "undisciplined" and "uninstructed," "inheriting"
the "stupidity of centuries of ignorant ancestors." At
school, they allegedly emitted a "pungent odor"—the
"fumes of New-England rum.". . .

Many Irish saw parallels between themselves as a degraded people and blacks in bondage. In Ireland, they had
identified themselves as the "slaves" of the British, and
many supported the abolition of slavery in the United
States. In 1842, thousands of them signed a petition that
declared: "Irishmen and Irishwomen! treat the colored
people as your equals, as brethren." But Irish sympathy for
black slaves seemed to disappear with the Atlantic crossing.
In America, many of them became antiblack. [Abolition-
ist and former slave] Frederick Douglass criticized the Irish
immigrants for abandoning the idea of "liberty" they nur-
tured in their homeland by becoming "the oppressors of
another race" in America. Irish freedom fighter Daniel
O'Connell shared Douglass's disappointment. Chastising
the immigrants for their racism, O'Connell declared: "It
was not in Ireland you learned this cruelty."

What the Irish had learned in America was actually a
painful and complex lesson. Stereotyped as ignorant and
inferior, they were forced to occupy the bottom rungs of
employment. In the South, they were even made to do the
dirty and hazardous jobs that masters did not want to as-

sign to their slaves. A planter told a northern visitor that he had hired an Irish gang rather than use his own slaves to drain a flooded area. "It's dangerous work," he explained, "and a negro's life is too valuable to be risked at it. If a negro dies, it's a considerable loss, you know." In the North, Irish repeatedly fought blacks for jobs as waiters and longshoremen. . . .

As they competed against blacks for employment, many Irish immigrants promoted their whiteness. "In a country of the whites where [white workers] find it difficult to earn a subsistence," they asked, "what right has the negro either to preference or to equality, or to admission?" The Irish were insisting on what historian David Roediger perceptively termed "their own whiteness and on white supremacy." Targets of nativist hatred toward them as outsiders, or foreigners, they sought to become insiders, or Americans, by claiming their membership as whites. A powerful way to transform their own identity from "Irish" to "American" was to attack blacks. Thus, blacks as the "other" served to facilitate the assimilation of Irish foreigners. . . .

"Down with the Nagurs!" "Let them go back to Africa, where they belong."

Irish antagonism toward blacks exploded during the Civil War. Many Irish were angry at President Abraham Lincoln for expanding the aims of the war to include emancipation. . . .

Irish Americans and Slavery

Condemning abolitionism as "Niggerology," many Irish immigrants were willing to support the war only to preserve the Union. They did not want to fight to free the slaves and thereby increase labor competition. "Let the niggers stay in the South!" Irish workers shouted. They had been warned by Democrats during the 1860 election: "Vote against Abraham Lincoln, or you will have negro labor dragging you from your free labor." "Let the four million of slaves in the South be set at liberty . . . and we should very soon have . . . a terrible conflict between white labor and black labor. . . . The unemployed slaves will be found among you in sufficient numbers to compete with you at your wharves and your docks, and in every branch of labor in which white people alone are now employed."

During the Civil War, New York Democratic politicians warned that the Republicans were willing to "spend" Irish blood to win the abolitionist war, and that freed blacks would be transported north to "steal the work and the bread of the honest Irish." Similarly, an Irish newspaper, the *Boston Pilot*, aroused the fears of its readers: "We have already upon us bloody contention between white and black labor. . . . The North is becoming black with refugee Negroes from the South. These *wretches* crowd our cities, and by overstocking the market of labor, do incalculable injury to white hands.". . .

Reacting to Irish hostility, blacks called their tormentors "white niggers." They resented being told by immigrants to leave the country of their birth and "go back" to Africa, a place they had never been. On one plantation, slaves mocked their Irish overseer by saying that an Irishman was "only a Negro turned inside out.". . .

Blacks complained that the Irish were taking jobs from them. "These impoverished and destitute beings, transported from the trans-Atlantic shores," a black observed, "are crowding themselves into every place of business and labor, and driving the poor colored American citizen out. Along the wharves, where the colored man once done the whole business of shipping and unshipping—in stores where his services were once rendered, and in families where the chief places were filled by him, in all these situations there are substituted foreigners. . . ."

As Americans, many blacks aimed nativist barbs

against the Irish foreigners. "Pat O'Flannagan does not have the least thing in the world against Jim from Dixie," a black observed, "but it didn't take Pat long after passing the Statue of Liberty to learn that it is popular to give Jim a whack." Blacks scornfully described the Irish as "hyphenates," and mocked their accent as such "a heavy brogue that it sounded as if they had marbles in their mouths." "It is to be regretted," black journalist John E. Bruce observed, "that in [America] where the outcasts—the scum of European society—can come and enjoy the fullest social and political privileges, the Native Born American with wooly hair and dark complexion is made the Victim . . . of Social Ostracism."

Finding Their Way: The Experiences of Irish Women

Kerby Miller and Paul Wagner

In this article Kerby Miller, professor of history at the University of Missouri at Columbia, and Paul Wagner, an Academy Award–winning producer-director of documentary films, explain why so many Irish women immigrated to America and what they did after they arrived. They write that the women saw little reason to stay in their homeland, adding that letters from women who had already immigrated often portrayed the United States as a land of opportunity. While male immigrants could usually find only low-paying jobs, females often worked in more comfortable conditions. The majority became domestic servants—housekeepers, nannies, and cooks—in the homes of the wealthy, where they could live in relative luxury while learning American ways from their employers. Many of the women sent some of the money they earned home to help their families or to pay for the immigration costs of other family members.

On New Year's Day, 1892, the first shipload of immigrants approached America's new reception facility at Ellis Island, in New York's harbor. The first person down the gangplank was an Austrian man. He politely stepped back in deference to a 15-year-old Irish girl named Annie Moore, making her the first immigrant to enter the United States

Kerby Miller and Paul Wagner, *Out of Ireland: The Story of Irish Emigration to America*. Washington, DC: Elliott & Clark Publishing, 1994. Copyright © 1994 by Kerby Miller and Paul Wagner. All rights reserved. Reproduced by permission of Rowman & Littlefield Publishing.

through Ellis Island. In at least two respects, this incident was symbolically appropriate.

First of all, it had been the Irish who primed American society for the waves of immigrants from many other lands who were to pass through Ellis Island into the New World.

And second, Annie Moore represented a feature of Irish immigration unique among all other immigrant groups. Of all the countries that sent immigrants to America in the late 19th and early 20th centuries, Ireland was the only one to send as many women as men. During several decades Irish female immigrants actually outnumbered males—in stark contrast to the migrations of Italians, Poles, Hungarians, and Greeks, among whom males overwhelmingly predominated.

In addition, the vast majority of Irish women who came to the United States did not come as wives or accompanied by parents. Nearly all of them were unmarried and traveling alone or in the company of sisters, cousins, or friends.

Two decades after the Famine, Alexander Sproule, a policeman in the northwestern Irish city of Londonderry, sent a plaintive letter to his brother in Ohio:

July 24, 1870

Dear Brother,

I have sorry news for you. On Thursday morning last, Ann, my eldest child, left here unknown to her mother and all, took all the money she could, leaving not the price of a loaf in the house, and started by steamer for Philadelphia. Perhaps you know some person in Philadelphia who could find her out. She is a smart, good girl—Whatever put this in her head? She is twenty-two years old, fair hair, clear skin, dark brown eyes, not tall. I know she is sorry for what she done. Please oblige me in a letter as we are in great trouble.

I am your affectionate brother

A. Sproule

Although the vast majority of Irish women emigrated with their parents' approval or encouragement, Ann Sproule is typical in her determination to leave Ireland and come to America. Indeed, the letters of female immigrants indicate that they were much more inclined than their menfolk to view emigration favorably—not as exile, but as opportunity or escape. But why did Ann Sproule and so many other young women come out of Ireland, and why did they perceive emigration in such positive terms?

One reason was that employment opportunities in the United States were often better for young, single Irishwomen than for their male relatives, especially as domestic servants in upper- and middle-class American homes. As Patrick McKeown, a day laborer from Ulster, reported rather enviously in a letter from Philadelphia dated 1894:

> *The most of all employments, although fairly paid, are very uncertain, except for hired or, as they are called here, living out girls. There is always a demand for them as few native girls care to go out as house servants. Therefore it is left to Irish girls. Their wages range from three to four dollars per week and keep. They seem to be the most successful and save more money than any other class, as they are at little or no expense and get a great many presents if they are fortunate in getting into a good house. In fact, you can hardly distinguish a girl going to her work from a prosperous merchant's wife or daughter!*

Few Options for Women in Ireland

In view of such opportunities, it was no wonder that poor Irishwomen flocked to the United States—and that domestic service was their most popular occupation. Some Irish American servants amassed savings of several thousand dollars or more before they quit paid employment and married.

By contrast, in post-Famine Ireland it was exceptionally difficult for a woman to find work or a husband.

Back in the late 18th and early 19th centuries, women in the Irish countryside had been economically important, earning much of the rent money through labor on neighboring farms or in spinning and other cottage industries. But by the mid–19th century, Irish domestic industries had declined dramatically, and the cities and towns offered women little employment or wretchedly low wages. Moreover, the shift in Ireland's post-Famine rural economy from crop tillage to livestock-raising sharply reduced opportunities for women to earn money in harvesting and other fieldwork. Irish parents still expected their daughters to work long, hard hours on farms or in shops—but without wages and with little hope for the future.

In late 19th-century Ireland, farmers' daughters could not marry men of their own choosing—and few were allowed to marry at all. Before the Famine, most Irish farmers had practiced what anthropologists call "partible inheritance": they had subdivided their holdings to provide farms for most or all of their sons, thus enabling them to marry and raise families of their own. This had made easy and early marriages possible, but it was a system that depended on farm families' willingness and ability to subsist largely on potatoes, the only crop that could provide sufficient nourishment to those who inhabited the smaller and smaller farms.

In this as in so many other respects, the Great Famine destroyed the old ways. The failure of the potato crop, plus the growing British demand for Irish cattle, persuaded farmers to keep the sizes of their landholdings and their cattle herds as large as possible. So, in the wake of the Famine, farmers adopted the pattern of impartible inheritance. Now parents willed their lands intact to only one son, and they usually required him to wait until he was middle-aged before they allowed him to take over the farm and marry.

Although most of the noninheriting sons emigrated, at least some could stay on as laborers on their more fortunate brothers' farms. But the daughters generally did not even have that option.

In addition, only those farmers' daughters whose fathers could give them dowries of money, land, or cattle were eligible to marry. Most farmers lacked sufficient capital to endow more than one of their daughters, which consigned the rest to spinsterhood in Ireland or to the emigrant ships. Under the dowry system Irish parents chose their daughters' husbands on the basis of economic calculations, not romantic notions. Instead of being free to marry for love, Irishwomen were usually "matched" with husbands who were many years older. By the 1920s the average marriage ages for men and women were 35 and 26, respectively. About one-fourth of Irish women aged 45 to 54 had never wed.

Finally, Irish parents' strict controls over their children's marriage chances were reinforced by the moral authority of the Catholic Church. In sermons and in schools, Irish priests and nuns admonished Irish youths to be dutiful and submissive, and to regard all potential occasions for romance as sinful, including even the crossroads dances that had once been a vital part of Irish rural life. Both priests and parents enforced a rigorous segregation on the young, separating males and females in church, in schools, in social clubs, even in the most public places. It was "a depressing sight," wrote one visitor to early 20th-century Ireland, "to witness lads and lasses walking on opposite sides of the roads and incurring the ban of the priest if they even talk to one another."

It is not surprising that young Irish people fled in droves from such restrictive conditions, lured by bright lights and prospects of comradeship and romance, as well as better work opportunities offered by American cities.

Young women, especially, left their homes for the social and economic independence that emigration promised. Their letters to Ireland only encouraged more of their dissatisfied sisters to follow their example. As one servant girl in New York City wrote to a female relation in County Wexford:

> *My dear cousin,*
>
> *I am sorry that the priest put such a hard penance on you. You will have to come to the country where there's love and liberty. It agrees very well with me. You would not think I have any beaux but I have a good many. I got half a dozen now. I have become quite a Yankee, and if I was at home the boys would all be around me. I believe I have got no more to say,*
>
> *From your affectionate friend.*
>
> *Mary Brown*

The Emigration of Mary Ann Rowe

Such a letter probably encouraged Mary Ann Rowe from the parish of Dunnamaggan in County Kilkenny, in southeastern Ireland, to make the trip to America.

Mary Ann Rowe's parents were comfortable, farming about 70 acres of rich land. They had no sons, but in 1887 Mary Ann's father promised his farm to her younger sister as a marriage dowry. Shortly thereafter, in the spring of 1888, Mary Ann emigrated to America and obtained work as a domestic servant in Dedham, Massachusetts, a small town near Boston. Later that year, she wrote a long letter to a close friend and former neighbor in Dunnamaggan:

> *October 29, 1888*
>
> *My dear friend,*
>
> *It is not through any lack of friendship that I stayed so long without writing to you. I do feel so bad when I go to write to home. I don't be the better of it for a long*

time. I would never have left poor Dunnamaggan if I only thought I would be so homesick. I cannot banish the thought of home out of my mind. There is not a night but I do be dreaming about you or someone from home. I dreamed last night that little John was dying. I fancied I was looking at him and had the pleasure of kissing him before he died. I hope and trust nothing is the matter with any of them.

Oh, when I look back to our former days! How often we spent an afternoon on Sunday chatting over something funny. When I think of poor little Ellen and Jeannie, how they used to come out in the fields to where we used to be working, and poor little Mary Anne, how she used to call "John, John, John." How nice we used to put in the Sunday together with the little ones around us.

Yet I am living with a very nice family here in Dedham, Massachusetts. They are very nice people. I would not be allowed to go outside to put out the clothes even when the dew was on the grass without rubber boots on me, my mistress is so very careful of me. And I am within two or three minutes walk from the church. There is a splendid church here in Dedham and three priests. I can go to mass every Sunday and to confession whenever I want to. Dedham is a very nice place and it is a country looking place—when you look around, there is nothing but trees.

I must draw to a close for the present by sending you all my best love.

I remain your affectionate friend until death.

Mary Ann Rowe

If the combination of her extreme homesickness for Ireland and her enthusiasm for her new life in America appears contradictory, it is also typical of many Irish women immigrants. Ultimately, it is also revelatory. For if their letters to friends and relatives in Ireland were tinged, or even awash, with homesickness for Ireland, they also were unambiguously positive about the relative merits of life in America.

On February 28, 1897, Mary Ann Rowe was married to Patrick J. Sutton, of Providence, Rhode Island. Tragically, one year later, she died shortly after giving birth to a baby boy. Still, her nine years of gainful employment, her social and economic independence, and her ability to marry a man of her own choosing were all positive aspects of a life she could never have led in Ireland.

"Undaunted and Unafraid"

In the late 19th century, Irish priests had counseled women against emigration, warning that America was a "godless" land where "rosy-faced, fair young girls, so pure, so innocent, so pious" would be "dragged down to shame and crime, and to an early and a dishonored grave." Nonetheless, such dire and lurid admonitions could never stem the flight of millions of young Irishwomen who sought, and usually found, love, liberty, and money in the United States.

As historian Hasta Diner explains, despite warnings and hazards, Irish female immigrants were "undaunted and unafraid." It was well they were so, for most of the money that financed post-Famine Irish emigration came not from Irish men in America but from Irish women. It came from the wages they sacrificed to send home to Ireland—while still saving enough to create their own dowries so as to attract husbands and establish families in the New World. Thus, Irish women abroad not only sustained the migration chains linking Ireland and the United States, but through their earnings and their children they helped lay the financial and human foundations of Irish America's future.

CHAPTER 3

Pain, Progress, and Assimilation

COMING TO AMERICA

The Irish in the
Civil War

Carl Wittke

Even though many of them feared emancipation because they knew freed slaves would compete with them for jobs, large numbers of Irish Americans fought for the Union cause in the Civil War. Meanwhile many Irish Americans who lived in the South fought on the Confederate side. In this selection noted historian Carl Wittke, who was a faculty member, dean, and vice president at Case Western Reserve University in Ohio, describes the contributions of Irish Americans in the war. He points out that they were known for their bravery, loyalty, and willingness to fight. While some of the actions of Irish Americans during the war were not exemplary—for example, Wittke describes their lack of discipline and a riot that was instigated by an Irish American mob—on the whole their contributions were admirable. Their willingness to fight also showed those Americans who had doubted their patriotism that Irish Americans were indeed loyal to their new homeland. Many historians see the Civil War as a turning point in the acceptance of the Irish as true Americans.

When [the Civil War] came the Irish did their full share. They had a conspicuous role in the Union army, which was "an amalgam of nations," and they also played an important part in the Confederate army. . . .

The number of Irish in the Union army has been estimated from 150,000 to 170,000, but the report of the

United States Sanitary Commission in 1869 placed the figure at 144,221 natives of Ireland, about five thousand
more than might have been expected in proportion to the
total Irish-American population. Of this number, 51,206
came from New York, 17,418 from Pennsylvania,12,041
from Illinois, 10,007 from Massachusetts, 8,129 from Ohio,
3,621 from Wisconsin, and 4,362 from Missouri.

Recruiting the Irish

In the excitement after the firing on Fort Sumter [the first
shot fired in the Civil War] many Irish enlisted. Like numerous others, they believed the war would be of short duration. As the fighting dragged on, "bounties" helped keep
the ranks filled, and during the last two years, many Irish
were drafted. The government carried on a systematic recruiting program among Irish immigrants. Many were en-
rolled immediately upon landing at Castle Garden. Within
twenty yards of this famous point of entry, there were two
large recruiting tents, bedecked with gay banners and
stocked with whiskey and food, where recruiting officers
offered liberal bounties for volunteers. As [nineteenth-
century Irish journalist] William H. Russell aptly put it,
many immigrants—Irish, Germans, and others—fought
not only *con amore* [with love] but also *pro dolore* (i.e., for
the dollar). Irishmen were persuaded that the war might
give them a chance to strike at England, and a number of
Irish outfits in the Civil War carried the green flag of Ireland with the American colors.

Federal agents, openly or secretly, recruited among pro-
spective Irish emigrants in Ireland, or lured Irishmen to
the United States with promises of jobs on the railroads
when their real purpose was to get them for the army. In
Dublin, Irishmen who were eager to enlist appealed to the
United States consul for free transportation to America.
Irish journals here and abroad denounced the recruiting

methods of "Federal agents," and the British government lodged formal protests in Washington. One of the most effective recruiting techniques used in this country was to promise a Catholic priest for every regiment. "You have fought nobly for the Harp and Shamrock," read one advertisement, "fight now for the Stars and Stripes. . . . Your adopted country wants you."

Courageous but Undisciplined

There is ample testimony from officers of every nationality and religious persuasion concerning the bravery and reckless courage of Irish soldiers. The New York *Times*, the New York *Herald*, and the New York *Tribune* carried editorials in praise of their loyalty. The Irish were steady and cool fighters, once the battle had begun, and they loved to fight. They frequently tossed away knapsacks and blankets, as they rushed into the wild and reckless charge fighting "like tigers." They were loyal to their outfits and to their officers, who knew how to handle them and spur them on, with matchless Irish oratory, to deeds of valor. The annals of the Civil War, both North and South, record scores of cases of personal gallantry. The losses among the Irish always were high, including officers.

The problem of discipline in the Union army was by no means limited to Irish soldiers, but the latter were prominently involved. The monotony of barracks life bored many Irishmen, and, while in camp, they proved hard to discipline. The Irish were better soldiers while fighting in offensive spurts than when forced to a sustained defensive. Irish soldiers, frequently intemperate and impetuous, were inclined to take to brawling when life got too dull. Excitable and often eloquently profane, companies of Irishmen were likely to settle their differences with their fists, especially after too much liquor. Conditions usually were worst right after the men received their pay. The chaplain of New York's Thirty-seventh Regiment recorded in his diary: "'Pay Day,' and of course drinking. Such a picture of hell I had never seen." Efforts were made to build morale by singing, celebrations of special holidays, races, dancing, and athletic contests, but frequently such festive occasions only added to the confusion. Serious trouble arose among recruits "from the roughs of the New York fire companies." Some of these outfits looked upon soldiering as a kind of continuous spree, and their infractions of discipline not only disturbed the army but the countryside where they were encamped. Pugnacious, quarrelsome, and often intemperate, they were also loyal to their own code of honor and, above all, were jovial and buoyant spirits. . . .

The Zouaves

According to the New York *Times* and the *Brooklyn Eagle*, the Irish Zouaves, or "Fire Zouaves," of New York were among the most undisciplined Irish units in the Union army. They marched off to war in fezzes, red firemen's shirts, and blue pants, and went into quarters at the Battery. There was so much trouble and drunkenness that seventy-five were dismissed from the service. The men climbed the gates at night, eluded the sentries, and disappeared into the city for a spree. New York papers charged them with cowardice at Bull Run, where relatively few soldiers seem to have distinguished themselves for bravery. It must be pointed out, however, that the Zouaves went to the front 850 strong and left 200 of their men as casualties on the field. New York firemen gave them a rousing welcome on their return to the city after the engagement.

At the first battle of Bull Run, the Irish charged the Confederates twice and then retreated with the rest. The Irish colonel of one regiment was court-martialed for lack of discipline, and he and his men were charged with drunkenness and brawling. A reporter from the *London*

Times accused [Thomas] Meagher's men [1] of running away from the battle, but there is evidence that the Sixty-ninth New York Regiment, described by one correspondent as "strolling, drunken vagabonds . . . picked up in the low groggeries of New York," "fought like tigers." No less a person than General William Tecumseh Sherman testified to their valor. Later, at Fredericksburg, Irish soldiers under Meagher, wearing green twigs in their hats, made six of the most heroic charges of the war. One regiment went in with 700 men and came out with 150. The dogged courage of the Irish at Antietam matched their reckless valor at Fredericksburg, and officers on both sides of the line testified to their courage. At Chancellorsville, the Irish brigade was virtually shot to pieces, and when Meagher resigned his command, only about 520 men were left of the five regiments of the original brigade.

It is not difficult to find evidences of insubordination, lack of discipline, brawling, and desertion among Irish soldiers alongside equally credible accounts of unusual devotion, valor, and fighting efficiency. The composition, organization, and administration of the Union army left much to be desired. Many officers of volunteer forces had no training and held their commissions because of political influence. Some were appointed by the governor of their state; others were elected by their own men. Old military companies whose objective always had been more social than military were now transferred *in corpore*, [as a body] into the Union army. The annals of the war contain many cases of incompetence, graft, cruelty, heavy drinking, rioting in camp, disobedience to discipline, and desertion and bounty jumping. A recruiting officer, paid so much a head for each man he enlisted, was not likely to be too discriminating. There can be no question that units

1. General Thomas Francis Meagher was the Irish-born commander of the 69th New York Regiment, which consisted primarily of Irish Americans.

like the Fire Zouaves and "Billy Wilson's boys" were notorious for rioting and lack of discipline. But trouble in many other units stemmed from poor organization, poor equipment, gouging of the men by sutlers who had the lucrative concessions at army camps, and incompetent and untrained officers.

Honoring Their War Heroes

As the war progressed, the Irish element in the United States had many occasions to honor their heroes. In 1862 and 1863, there were numerous ceremonies for the bestowal of swords, medals, and gifts such as saddles and gold spurs to Irish military leaders. . . .

With their innate love of pageantry, the Irish arranged parades to see their soldiers off to the front and to give them a hero's welcome upon their return. When the famous Sixty-ninth New York Regiment departed in the spring of 1861, they were escorted by Hibernian Benevolent and other Irish societies, several fire companies, Irish police, and the "Exile Club," and in the parade there was a wagon decorated with banners and the slogan, "Remember Fontenoy."[2] Colonel [Michael] D. Corcoran received a large bunch of shamrocks, and the steamer which carried his troops down the harbor pulled out to the booming of cannon and with the lusty cheers of hundreds of New York Irishmen resounding in their ears. . . .

The Draft Riots

The ineradicable black spots upon the Irish escutcheon during the war were the brutal draft riots of 1863 in New York City. The draft law was opposed in other parts of the nation and by other nationality groups, and others besides Irishmen participated in the disgraceful New York riots. The

2. In 1745, at the Battle of Fontenoy in France, the French army and an Irish brigade defeated British and Dutch forces.

Irish, however, played such a predominant role that the result was a bitter anti-Irish reaction throughout the country.

In comparison with World War I and II, the draft law of the Civil War was clearly unfair. It provided that a draftee could escape military service by paying $300 in cash or by furnishing a substitute. The poor had good reason to complain that the law demanded "Three Hundred Dollars or Your Life." Substitutes became "a marketable commodity," and brokerage firms were established to furnish men who were willing to go to war for a price. The draft, which was contrary to American tradition, was especially unpopular with the foreign-born, who had left Europe to escape military service. To the Irish, conscription was doubly objectionable. It came almost simultaneously with emancipation, and the Irishman had no stomach for fighting for his Negro competitor in the labor market. The machinery for administering the draft, hastily improvised, proved inadequate and lent itself to manipulation for political or personal favoritism.

Opposition to the draft appeared in a number of states. There were disturbances in New England, Pennsylvania, Ohio, New Jersey, Illinois, and Wisconsin. Two marshals were attacked in Boston, hardware stores were robbed of knives and guns, and several persons were killed. A meeting at St. Mary's Institute on July 13, 1863, ended with cheers for [president of the Confederacy] Jefferson Davis. In Rutland, Vermont, Irish quarry workers drove off the enrolling officers with clubs and stones. In Pottsville, Pennsylvania, armed Irish miners resisted the draft. In Troy, New York, a Negro church was torn down and a local newspaper attacked during a draft riot. Order was finally restored by the local priest and the militia from Albany. In Ozaukee County, Wisconsin, in November, 1862, Germans had threatened to lynch several Republicans; in Milwaukee, both Irish and Germans opposed conscription;

and there were disturbances in parts of Indiana and in the Irish mining section around Dubuque, Iowa.

Such incidents, however, were completely overshadowed by what happened in New York in July, 1863. Before the war, New York firms had many business connections with

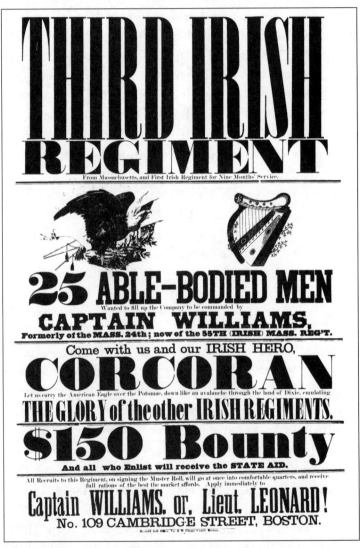

A Civil War–era recruiting poster urges Irish Americans to enlist in the Union army.

the South, and there was much sympathy for the Confederacy. At one point during the war, the mayor talked about having the city "secede." In 1863, Negroes were used as strikebreakers against longshoremen and stevedores whose wages were less than $1.50 a day. The draft was unfairly administered by Republican officials in New York City and Brooklyn, and, in one respect, the draft riots represented a revolt of the poor, who did the fighting, against the "shoddy aristocracy," who did the profiteering. The New York *Herald* described the draft riots as "a popular outbreak inspired by a burning sense of wrong," and the New York *World* commented that apparently "poor men refused to be forced into a war" which was mismanaged and perverted to partisan purposes. Bishop [John] Hughes wrote his friend, the Secretary of State, that the basic cause of the riots was the attempt "to make black labor equal to white labor . . . with the difference that black labor shall have local patronage over the toil of the white man."

Both Governor Horatio Seymour and Mayor Fernando Wood denounced conscription as unconstitutional. Several New York papers helped stir the Irish to fury. Everyone who was "opposed to the war for the negro . . . and in favor of the rights of the poor" was invited to a mass meeting, and the mayor used the occasion to demand an armistice and a peace conference. Of the Irish papers, the *Irish-American* and the *Metropolitan Record* were the most inflamatory. The latter, although it no longer assumed to speak for Bishop Hughes, carried at the masthead the words "A Catholic Family Paper." Editorially, it denounced the draft as "military despotism" and a deadly blow to popular liberties, made ugly comparisons between the administration and Russia's "fiendish rule in Poland," referred to good Americans led in chains by "a minority President," and virtually counseled insurrection. The paper pointed out that whereas it cost a white man $300 to buy exemption from the draft, in the South a Negro could not be bought for less than $2,000. When the editor finally was arrested and charged with inciting his readers to resist the draft, he was defended by Charles O'Conor and Charles Donohue and escaped conviction on a technicality.

The drawings in New York City began on Saturday, July 11, 1863. Republican provost marshals were in charge, and most of the names drawn were those of poor workers, many of them Irish, who could neither pay $300 nor procure substitutes. Over the week end, the Irish sections of the city were seething with angry charges of discrimination and by Monday the steam exploded. Gangs of rioters marched to Central Park, stormed and burned the draft office, beat the superintendent of police, raided houses on Lexington Avenue, destroyed a colored orphan asylum which housed two hundred children between the ages of two and twelve, drove innocent Negroes in panic through the streets, and hanged several. Chinese, considered close enough in color to Ethiopians, also were attacked. Horsecars were held up, stores and homes pillaged, and telegraph wires cut. For three days, the city was terrorized by a brutal, frenzied mob. Estimates of the total dead fluctuated wildly from eighteen to seventy-four. Among them were some Irish and Germans. Finally, the Provost Marshal announced in the newspapers that the draft was suspended, and a regiment was brought in from Meade's army at Gettysburg to restore order. On the fourth day, when the worst was over, Archbishop Hughes summoned the faithful to his home, and on the following day addressed a crowd of three thousand from his balcony. Like scores of other priests, he demanded an end to the disorder.

Archbishop Hughes' address was his last public speech. He died shortly thereafter. In August, 1862, upon his return from Europe, he had urged volunteering, but also had recommended conscription if this means was necessary to bring the war to a quick end. On July 15, 1863, Hughes explained to the New York *Herald* that he had never favored "coercive conscription" but had recommended that "the people of the North, who stand by the Federal government should demand conscription by their own voluntary choice and act. This would be their own system of volunteering." In one of his sermons, he had urged "the people to rise and ask the government to draft them" and had said that "those who are wealthy and cannot go themselves can provide subsitutes."

Hughes' address to his parishioners was a masterpiece of diplomacy. He referred to suffering and oppression in Ireland and spoke flatteringly of his Irish countrymen. He stressed the heavy loss of life and property in the riots, but carefully refrained from accusing his listeners. He pleaded for constitutional methods of redress and concluded by advising his audience to go calmly to their homes and "not to give up your principles and convictions, but keep out of the crowd in which immortal souls are launched into eternity without a moment's notice." The speech was shrewd, effective, and interspersed with references to Irish patriots and exiles and John Bull [the British equivalent of Uncle Sam]. One senses that the prelate realized he had to handle the crowd with all the skill he could muster. The comments of the New York press varied. Some were sharply critical. William Cullen Bryant's New York *Evening Post* pointed out that all Irishmen should not be condemned because of the misdeeds of the worst element among them. Many Irish had refused to join the rioters. Two of New York's Irish wards remained quiet, and their colored residents were not disturbed. In one ward, Irish porters and laborers formed a guard to beat off the mob. The police, many of whom were Irish, made a reasonably good record in trying to maintain law and order. The New York *Times* reported that one Irishman had proposed that his countrymen raise $50,000 to rebuild the Negro orphanage which Irish vandals had destroyed.

The majority of the rioters were Irish, and there would have been even more brutality except for the intervention of the priests. Papers like the Cincinnati *Catholics Telegraph* denounced the riot and every form of resistance to the draft. The *Metropolitan Record*, whose inflammatory editorials helped bring on the riot, editorially condemned the "revolting, fiendish, cowardly, cruel" treatment of "the poor unfortunate negroes" and argued that "a superior race should disdain to vent their passions on an inferior one," especially Negroes, who were "the footballs of every party." George Templeton Strong [diarist whose diary covers much of the nineteenth centry] recorded in his diary that "the rabble was perfectly homogeneous. Every brute in the drove was pure Celtic-hod-carrier or loafer." With equal fury, he denounced "the low Irish women . . . stalwart young vixens and withered old hags . . . all cursing the 'bloody draft' and egging on their men to mischief.". . .

The Irish in the Confederate Army

Below Mason and Dixon's line, the Irish had rallied to the defense of the South as readily as their northern brothers had to the Union cause. In both sections, the Church tried to remain aloof from the bitter internecine struggle. A number of priests privately expressed opposition to slavery, but were careful not to ally themselves with the antislavery movement. Southern Irishmen, even more than those in the North, feared the effect of emancipation on white labor.

There were nearly 85,000 Irish in the South when the war began. The majority lived in the four states of Louisiana, Missouri, Tennessee, and Virginia. Charleston, South Carolina, had about 3,300 Irish; New Orleans nearly 25,000 in 1850. The majority of southern Irish favored state rights and hated "the dirty nigger-loving Yanks." The suspension of work on levees and railroads in the lower Mississippi Valley during the war made jobless Irishmen eager to enlist. On several occasions, southern and northern Irish met face to face in combat. "Everywhere in the Confederate States," reported the *Southern Watchman* of Athens, Georgia, "they have been among the foremost to volunteer, and among the most liberal in contributing to the comfort of the brave soldiers in the field." Irish blacksmiths and machinists were in great demand in the southern army, and Confederate generals spoke highly of Irish soldiers. Some preferred them as clean, spirited, fearless fighters who were loyal to their leaders and whose irrepressible sense of humor did not fail them even in moments of greatest danger.

Roberdeau Wheat's Batallion, called "The Tigers" and "The Irish Tartars," was a famous unit from Louisiana. At Fredericksburg, Georgia Irishmen defended St. Mary's Hill against Meagher's Irish from the North. The Emmet Guards and the Montgomery Guards were companies from Richmond, Virginia. The Emerald Guards of the Eighth Alabama Regiment consisted largely of Irish laborers. They wore dark green uniforms and carried a shamrock and harp emblazoned on one side of their Confederate flag. A number of Louisiana companies were composed of Irish military organizations that had joined the Confederate army as units. There were other Irish outfits from Tennessee, and one company of Irish Confederates came from Wilmington, North Carolina. The Meagher Guards of Charleston, South Carolina, changed its name after the firing on Fort Sumter to the Emerald Light Infantry. The Fifth Confederate Regiment, commanded by General Patrick Cleburne of Arkansas and composed largely of Irish, fought gallantly at Missionary Ridge [in Tennessee]. One of John Mitchel's sons was killed at Fort Sumter, another at Gettysburg. General Joseph Finnigan defended

Florida against Union attacks. David Flannery of Limerick was superintendent of telegraphs between Memphis and New Orleans. Lee's Irish orderly, Bryan, had an excellent reputation as a good forager and cook. Michael Quinn was chief engineer on the *Alabama*. It must be added that there were also Irish deserters from both Confederate and Union armies, and some were court-martialed for breaches of discipline or cowardice.

Among the distinguished southern Irish military leaders, General Patrick Cleburne, an Irish Episcopalian, was outstanding. In Ireland he had been apprenticed to a druggist. When he failed the qualifying examination, he joined the British army. In 1849, he came to the United States to resume work as a druggist, first in Cincinnati, then in Arkansas. In 1856, he was admitted to the bar. Originally a Whig, he became a Democrat during the Know-Nothing days. He was an impulsive, generous Irishman with remarkable oratorical gifts, and always spoke with an Irish accent. Though he lived in a slave state, he owned no slaves, and in 1864 he advocated arming Negroes for the Confederate army and giving them their freedom upon their discharge from service. Cleburne had a brother in each of the opposing armies. His brilliant military record made him a major general in 1862. He distinguished himself at Chickamauga and Missionary Ridge and became known as "the Stonewall Jackson of the West." He was killed, when not quite thirty-eight, at Franklin, and buried near Columbia, Tennessee.

The Confederacy, like the Union government, dispatched special envoys to Ireland to propagandize for the southern cause. Lieutenant James L. Capston and Father John Bannon, a St. Louis priest and Confederate chaplain, as well as several other native Irishmen described as "long residents of the United States," went to Ireland to stop recruiting for the Union army. Their speeches emphasized the Know-Nothing outrages and insisted that Irish Catholics could not feel at home in the northern states. A poster displayed in Cork and Limerick carried such phrases as "The Blessed Host Scattered on the Ground! Benediction Veil Made a Horse Cover of! All the Sacred Vessels Carried Off!" and "The Priest Imprisoned and Afterwards Exposed on an Island to Alligators and Snakes!" Father Bannon lectured widely in Ireland, wrote under the name of "Sacerdos," circulated handbills among parish priests to prove that American Know-Nothings were the descendants of [British and persecutor of the Irish Oliver] Cromwell, and repeated the familiar stories of the desecration of Catholic Churches in the United States. Confederate propaganda undertook to prove that, like Ireland, the South was fighting for self-government, and Confederate agents quoted [Irish patriots] William Smith O'Brien, John Mitchel, John Martin, and other Irish exiles to support their argument. Confederate broadsides also contrasted the materialism of the North with the Christian civilization of the South. In 1864, Bishop [P.N.] Lynch of Charleston was appointed by [Confederate] President [Jefferson] Davis as Confederate commissioner to the Papal States, but the Vatican was careful to receive him only as a bishop and not as a representative of the Confederacy.

The New York Draft Riots

New York Times

In the first years of the Civil War, men enlisted for each side in such high numbers that a draft was not necessary. However, as the war dragged on the number of soldiers who signed up began to wane, so in March 1863 Congress passed the Conscription Act, which required all able-bodied men to enlist. The act contained a clause that stated that draftees could avoid going to war if they hired a substitute or paid a three-hundred-dollar fee. This clause angered those men who lacked the money to do either of these things. They claimed that Congress was favoring those with money while condoning the deaths of thousands of poor men. Several protests against the draft occurred, the most violent taking place in July 1863 in New York. The article below is an excerpt from a *New York Times* article written on July 15, 1863, which describes an attack on draft offices. Large numbers of men from railroad companies and foundries stopped working and persuaded or forced workers from other businesses to join their protest; soon the mob grew from about sixty people to more than five hundred. They rushed into draft offices, destroyed paperwork and furniture, and set several offices on fire. A number of men were also attacked. The unnamed author writes that the city and federal authorities were not prepared for the riot and could not control it.

The initiation of the draft on Saturday in the Ninth Congressional District was characterized by so much order and

New York Times, "The Mob in New York," vol. 12, July 15, 1863.

good feeling as to well nigh dispel the foreboding of tu-
mult and violence which many entertained in connection
with the enforcement of the conscription in this City. Very
few, then, were prepared for the riotous demonstrations
which yesterday from 10 in the morning until late at night
provided almost unchecked in our streets. The authorities
had counted upon more or less resistance to this measure
of the Government after the draft was completed, and the
conscripts were required to take their place in the ranks,
and at that time they would have been fully prepared to
meet it, but no one anticipated resistance at so early a stage
in the execution of the law, and, consequently, both the
City and National authorities were totally unprepared to
meet it. The plotters of the riot knew this, and in it they
saw their opportunity. We say plotters of the riot, for it is
abundantly manifest that the whole affair was concocted
on Sunday last by a few wire-pullers, who, after they saw
the ball fairly in motion yesterday morning prudently kept
in the background. Proof of this is found in the fact that
as early as 9 o'clock, some laborers employed by two or
three railroad companies, and in the iron foundries on the
eastern side of the City, formed in procession in the
Twenty-second Ward, and visited the different workshops
in the upper wards, where large numbers were employed,
and compelled them by threats in some instances, to cease
their work. As the crowd augmented, their shouts and disorderly demonstrations became more formidable. The
number of men, who thus started out in their career of violence and blood, did not probably at first exceed three-
score. Scarcely had two dozen names been called, when a
crowd, numbering perhaps 500, suddenly made an irrup-
tion in from of the building, (corner of Third-avenue and
Forty-sixth street), attacking it with clubs, stones, brick-
bats and other missiles. The upper part of the building was
occupied by families who were terrified beyond measure at

the smashing of the windows, doors, and furniture. Following these missiles, the mob rushed furiously into the office on the first floor, where the draft was going on, seizing the books, papers, records, lists, &c., all of which they destroyed, except those contained in a large iron safe. The drafting officers were set upon with stones and clubs, and, with the reporters for the Press and others, had to make a hasty exit through the rear. They did not escape scatheless, however, as one of the enrolling officers was struck a savage blow with a stone, which will probably result fatally, and several others were injured.

From the above it will be seen that the drawing by Provost Marshal Jenkins did not commence punctually at 9 o'clock, as was intended. Intimations had been received that a riot was probable, and Acting Assistant Provost Marshal General Nugent was applied to for a force which would be sufficient to preserve the peace. At ten o'clock, however, no other response had been made to this application than the arrival of a dozen policemen and Provost Marshal Jenkins decided to resume the drawing. The wheel was placed prominently upon the table, the blind-folded man stood beside it, the man whose duty it was to turn the wheel was ready, and Mr. Jenkins announced that the draft, which was begun on Saturday, would be concluded. At this time, there were about two hundred persons present, and during the twenty minutes before the riot was inaugurated, they freely made use of excited and threatening language. These ruffians did not hesitate at all about joining the main body of the rioters as soon as they arranged themselves before the building, and their exit was the signal for the attack, which commenced with a volley of stones. When the office had been cleared of the officers and other persons, many of the more excited of the rioters rushed in and played instant havoc with machinery and demolishing the furniture and papers. The books, lists and records, and blanks were dragged into the street, torn into fragments, and scattered everywhere with loud imprecations and savage yells. The men seemed to be excited beyond expression, and in their futile efforts to wrench open the iron safe which contained the names of the drafted, gave themselves wholly to devilish rage and fury.

The Mob Sets Fire to the Draft Office

The destruction of the material in the office was hardly accomplished when smoke was discovered to be issuing from the rest of the room and this evidence of the building being on fire was received with vociferous shouts, and other indications of delight. As the flames gradually increased, the passions of the mob grew deeper, and their yelling and brandishing of clubs and threatening of everybody connected with enforcement of the draft was more emphatic. Some of the crowd supposed that the Enrolling officers had secreted themselves in the upper part of the building, and notwithstanding the fact that women and children were known to occupy the upper floors, the cowardly wretches threw stones and other missiles into the windows.

Fearing that these poor people would either be burned to death or maimed by these projectiles, Deputy Provost-Marshal Edward S. Vandderfore bravely stepped out to the front, and assuring the rioters that they had utterly destroyed all the drafting paraphenalia, requested them to withdraw, or to do something to prevent the destruction of the helpless women and children. Suspecting from his uniform that he was one of the drafting officers, one of the rioters seized him and struck him. Mr. Vanderfore merely shook off his assailant and in a pacific manner, renewed his request when the action of the fire attracted the attention of the rioters and a number of the men grabbed him with their hands, with stones and . . . because he could not resist them, he withdrew to the place where the police were posted. The rioters followed him with great clubs, and the men, who were desperate, beat him upon the body and head. His head was so badly bruised that blood flowed profusely, when he was thrown down and kicked. He afterward escaped by the aid of the police and one or two of his friends, but the rioters followed him, striking him with clubs. He is so badly injured that there is but little probability of his recovery.

Meantime the fire spread from the enrolling office to the adjoining buildings, and the entire block was consumed.

The Irish Style in Politics

William V. Shannon

William V. Shannon, who was a journalist, professor, and ambassador, died in 1988. In the following selection Shannon describes how Irish Americans started grassroots neighborhood campaigns that eventually brought them to political power in many cities. They created a political "machine" that provided favors to constituents in return for votes. Shannon explains that Irish Americans managed to maintain control of some cities for years by engaging in both honest practices and in other techniques that were not so honest, such as graft and nepotism.

In the decades after the Civil War, the Irish developed their characteristic style in American politics. . . .

The Irish made their big move into American politics at a time when both the theory and the practice of politics were at a peculiarly low ebb. The nation's earliest political tradition originated in the seventeenth and eighteenth centuries among the planters of Virginia and the Puritan aristocrats and merchants of New England. This tradition held that politics is a serious affair worthy of the attention of the best class of men. The governing of mankind, in this view, is an enterprise too important for the natural leaders of society, the men of property and education, to leave to intermediaries and underlings. Washington, Jefferson, Madison, [American statesman John] Jay, and the

William V. Shannon, *The American Irish*. New York: Macmillan, 1963.

Adamses who organized the American Revolution, wrote the Constitution, and founded the national government shared this viewpoint. They were never guilty of the fatuous maxim "It's just politics."

The merchants and industrial entrepreneurs who came to the fore in the early nineteenth century produced a different theory of politics. What has become known as the Whig view of government contended "that government is best which governs least." The primary task of politics was to make government a tidy, efficient housekeeper. The business community developed the comfortable and useful mythology that social conflict was unreal, that the interests of employers and workers, of farmers and city consumers, of businessmen and customers were actually identical. Since this was true, the two-party system was more a convenience than a necessity. If there were no social conflicts, then party warfare was devoid of meaning. Party affiliations could be regarded as matters of sentiment, as eccentric vestiges of the past rather than reflections of vital interests. By 1870 this view had become dominant in writings and discussions of politics among educated easterners. The "independent voter" who rejected both parties and chose the better man regardless of label was extolled as the best voter. In these years the business community not only attracted the best talents but also imposed upon politics its standards of efficiency and economical operation as ends in themselves rather than as means in attaining the larger public welfare. "Politics" became a naughty word associated with corrupt schemers and raids on the treasury. During the late Victorian age, the genteel tradition was as supreme in American politics as it was in literature. . . .

[American author and minister Edward Everett] Hale and other reformers [who criticized this style of government] were in the minority as the extreme individualist, antigovernment views of [philosopher] Herbert Spencer became the vogue. The chief exponent of the majority viewpoint was E.L. Godkin, long-time editor of the New York *Evening Post* and of the *Nation* magazine. Although monopolies, slums, child labor, periodic mass unemployment, and other evils ravaged society, Godkin and other writers on politics devoted most of their attention to the introduction of the civil service system and to thinking of ways to lure educated men into politics. Godkin wrote in "The Duty of Educated Men in a Democracy": "We should probably, in a college-graduate government, witness the disappearance from legislation of nearly all acts and resolutions which are passed for what is called 'politics'; that is, for the purpose of pleasing certain bodies of voters, without any reference to their value as contributions to the work of government."

It is not astonishing that with this narrow, uncomprehending theory of politics in the ascendancy, the masses of immigrants crowding into the growing cities had to develop their own political institutions and their own political ethic. The immigrant laborer desperate for a job to feed his family, the immigrant family quarreling with the landlord, the widowed mother deprived of her income, the injured workman, the sweatshop employee, and the truant boy in trouble with the police needed someone or some agency more compassionate and helpful than routine "good government," no matter how purified by civil service reform or economically run by college graduates. Moreover, the immigrants perceived that when government at different levels did exercise positive power, it was usually on behalf of businessmen by granting land subsidies to railroad companies or using police to break strikes. . . .

The Political Machine

The Irish, the most numerous and advanced section of the immigrant community, took over the political party (usually the Democratic Party) at the local level and converted it into virtually a parallel system of government. The network of party clubhouses and the hierarchy of party committees with a citywide leader or "boss" at the apex constituted a "shadow government," a supplementary structure of power that performed some functions more vital than those of the nominal, legal government. The main objective of the party, of course, was to capture control of the city government, but even when the party was out of office, it could continue to function. It had revenue from the "tax" it levied upon saloons, houses of prostitution, gamblers, and contractors. Out of these funds, the party machine could provide the food and coal it gave to those who were destitute. It could finance the young lawyers who interceded in court for the delinquent, wrote letters home to the old country for the illiterate, and intervened at city hall for those bewildered by the regulations and intricacies of the government. It could pay for the torchlight parades, the children's picnics, and the one-day excursion trips up the river or to the beach which brought recreation and a touch of color to the lives of working-class families.

When the machine was in office, it could provide that most precious of all commodities: a job. Public construction work was one of the major sources of jobs and income. When reform administrations were in power, they cut back on construction to save money and reduce the tax rate. When the machine was in power, it expanded construction, building courthouses and schoolhouses, paving more streets, digging more subways, and erecting new bridges. The politicians at the top liked building programs because they could collect bribes from those who received the contract, make "a killing" on the sale of the land on the basis of their advance knowledge, profit by writing the insurance on the project, and sometimes organize a sand-and-gravel company and get cut into the actual construction as a subcontractor. This was "honest graft," sometimes known as "white graft" to distinguish it from the "dirty graft" collected via the police department from the underworld. The contractors liked this expansive attitude toward public works projects because it increased their business, and so did the carpenters, plumbers, plasterers, and other skilled craftsmen. But, most of all, the newest and least skilled of the immigrants were enthusiastic because these projects enabled them to find work as laborers. Since, at the outset of their life in America, they were fitted only to do pick-and-shovel work, they were peculiarly dependent upon the machine and its free-and-easy spending of public money. No number of exposés by citizens' committees and good government groups of graft, payroll padding, and excessive spending on public projects shook their loyalty to the machine. If there were no "corrupt machine," they reasoned, there might not be any building projects, and if there were no projects to work on, how would they earn enough to live? Padded payrolls were better than no payrolls. Since the city usually needed the building or public improvement, it was not easy for critics to demonstrate to working-class voters what harm had been done.

Building the Machine

The political machines the Irish built in most of the major cities of the North and Midwest developed out of the block and the neighborhood. Family friendships and neighborhood loyalties were the basis of power. The boyhood gangs with their emphasis on loyalty and cohesiveness provided the morale and the habits of mind that were easily transmuted, in adult years, into the rationale of the machine. The citywide leaders, the ward and precinct captains, and the rank-and-file members of the party machines developed a set of political ethics and an attitude toward politics and power that were strikingly different from those of the native middle-class code. The Irish viewed municipal politics not as a conflict over how to obtain the best government at the lowest cost but as a struggle for power among competing groups.

The earliest leaders organized the Irish voters as a battering ram to break the power of a hostile majority. They put an end to elementary forms of discrimination such as the exclusive use of the King James Bible in the schools and the assignment of Protestant chaplains to Catholic inmates of hospitals, jails, and charitable institutions. Next, they fought for the appointment of Irish as schoolteachers and as policemen and firemen. Finally, they sought to take all political power into their own hands.

In the course of this struggle for power, the Irish community evolved an attitude of tolerant acceptance of political corruption. This was neither cynicism nor hypocrisy; rather it was close to a straightforward acceptance of graft as necessary and inevitable. Graft was part of the operating compromise between the formal rules of the political system and the facts of life as it was actually lived. Corruption was often viewed as a primitive mechanism for redistributing the wealth because, as people said, "at least it keeps the money in circulation." The Irish and their allies among other immigrants had the attitude typical of those who comprise a client group and not a ruling class. For a long period, they were people who had statute without status, power without responsibility. Only gradually did the social discipline grow to match the power, and only when that happened did the majority detach themselves from the values of the political machine.

Politics as a Career

For individual Irish, politics was an attractive career. Since newly naturalized voters were usually more willing to give their votes to another "son of the old country" than to a native-born candidate, politics was the only major profession in which it was an asset rather than a drawback to be an immigrant. Politics, like baseball, prizefighting, and the Church, was a career open to talents, a path of social mobility for the ambitious sons of impoverished families.

This Irish concept of politics as another profession—practical, profitable, and pursued every day in the year—diverged sharply from the ordinary civic code that draped politics in the mantle of "public service." According to the genteel tradition, the holding of office was an ephemeral activity; it might be thought of as an accident comparable to a call for jury service that might befall any citizen. For those who regarded the main business of America as business, service in a political office represented a sacrifice. In the Irish community, there was no talk of duty or sacrifice. Nor did those who gave their time to politics regard the holding of public office as an interlude or an accident. Politics was their career. Like every other profession, it was expected to reward its practitioners with money, prestige and, if possible, security. It was generally expected that a politician would make money out of his office, collaterally if not directly, and that if he lost he would be "taken care of" in a sinecure.

Helping Out Friends and Neighbors

Since Irish politicians were of working-class origin, they entered public office trailing long strings of needy relatives. Because the public payroll was the politician's only resource, he was expected to use it to succor his family and dependents. The result was the nepotism so frequently and so futilely condemned by civic reformers. This nepotism was usually controlled by some sense of official responsibility. A halfwit or a drunkard would not be placed in a responsible job, but some other provision might be made for him. Indeed, some other provision had to be made for him.

(What of his wife and children? If no one else would hire him, what politician would take the responsibility of sending "your own flesh-and-blood" to the relief rolls or the gutter?)

Nepotism had old-country roots. For generations, each immigrant who "went out to the States" had a fixed responsibility to send back money to pay for the subsequent passage of one of his brothers or sisters. In many families the oldest son came first, paid the fare of the next oldest who paid for the next, and so on. This recruitment practice was known as "sending for a greenhorn." The immigrant was also morally obligated to find jobs here for his relatives and for as many of his neighbors from the old country as he could. In this way, the kitchens of many a mansion and the police, fire, and streetcar departments of many a city were regularly staffed. . . .

It is a short step from neighborliness to nepotism. However much such nepotism might be deplored, it could not be otherwise when men were bred from childhood to an urgent and overriding feeling of family duty and parochial loyalty.

Politics as a career not only required a minimum of education, preparation, and money; it also had the advantage over competing occupations that for the few who had the requisite talents it produced its rewards relatively quickly. In this respect, politics had the same appeal as professional athletics. It is significant how many politicians achieved power at an early age. James Curley was a congressman at thirty-six and mayor of Boston at thirty-nine; Joseph Tumulty of Jersey City became President [Woodrow] Wilson's chief aide at thirty-three; Alfred E. Smith and James J. Walker were floor leaders in the New York legislature while still in their thirties. Charm, boldness, energy, a quick mind and a fluent tongue brought young politicos to the top; unlike careers in business and the professions, politics required neither long years of saving and scrimping nor any exact training.

The Political Psychology

The swiftness of success was probably important in shaping the psychology of many of these political leaders. Because of family necessity, a youth would become a part-time wage earner—a newsboy or bootblack or messenger—and thereby be forced into a premature maturity. He found himself drawn out of his own neighborhood, which up until then had seemed exciting and satisfying, and into the larger world. Back on his home block, a dime had been a fortune, pot roast was a Sunday treat, and beer was his father's luxury after a ten- or twelve-hour shift. But in the brighter, faster-moving world in which he now entered, the youth encountered men who wore silk shirts, ate steak for lunch, and seemed to possess large sums of money. The ambitious adolescent went through several kinds of experience simultaneously. He became aware that, in material terms, there were ways of life better than that of his own family; he felt the first pangs of the adult desires for freedom, sex, and money; he felt the sharp twinges of class envy and personal hope. For many youths this accelerated coming of age in a materialistic society must have had permanently distorting effects. They could see that ordinary occupations—tending a machine or pounding a beat, pressing pants or making them, selling spools of thread or pecks of potatoes—were not going to bring quick success. For those with the right blend of imagination, audacity, and style, politics was the obvious answer.

A politician with this psychological background was obviously more vulnerable to the temptations to dishonesty in office than one who enjoyed a more secure and orderly transition through adolescence into adulthood. During the psychological crisis which shaped his personal sense of identity, certain material objects and a certain style of life obtained an excessive hold on his imagination. The keener his imagination and the better his mind, then the greater the potentiality for a certain kind of tragedy. The routine wardheeler may graft on a petty scale because the ethical code of his community condones it, but the abler and more ambitious politico grafts not only because it is permissible but also because he is subject to all the pressures and insecurities of the parvenu. Having entered politics to raise himself from the ranks of laborers and hodcarriers, he travels a long way vertically in a larger society which recognizes material success as its chief criterion. To move in the social circles and live in the manner which he desired took more money than the politician could possibly acquire honestly. This was true even though he remained within the orbit of the rich and successful of his own kind. The races at Saratoga, the summer house at the seashore, daughter's grand piano—all these and other tangibles of success cost money. One does not have to join the Four Hundred [an exclusive social set] to live beyond one's means. An Alfred E. Smith or Joseph Tumulty would have a code of rigid personal honesty or develop a set of social ideals to protect himself against the grafter's temptation, but the more typical politician could not avoid giving the wrong answer to the uneasy question: If it was not to travel with these people and live this way, then why did he ring doorbells, run for alderman, or go into politics in the first place?

Those who entered politics as a means of rapid personal advancement were acting from a motive that neither the theory of the founders of the nation nor the theory of the late nineteenth century middle classes had taken into account or could accommodate. Moreover, Irish machine politics was carried on in an intellectual void. It was the intuitive response to practical necessities and unrelated to any comprehensive theory of politics and society. Until the emergence of [*Collier's* magazine editor] Finley Peter Dunne's "Mr. Dooley"[1] in the late 1890's and the realistic investigations of politics by [investigative journalist] Lincoln Steffens and other muckraking magazine writers early in this century, the code by which the Irish politicians and their mass of supporters lived and governed remained unarticulated and undefended. As a result, the larger society outside the Irish community looked upon the party bosses as grotesque; politics seemed a morality play in which, despite frequent scandals and exposures, vice always triumphed; and the gloomier observers despaired of democracy. But for the Irish, politics was a functioning system of power and not an exercise in moral judgment. While E.L. Godkin and Henry Adams despaired of the American experiment, the Irish took over City Hall.

1. a fictional Irish saloonkeeper who gave his opinion on many contemporary issues

Crowded Conditions: A Firsthand View of a Tenement

William Dean Howells

Novelist and *Harper's Magazine* editor William Dean Howells was a member of the school of realism, which means that his desire was to show life not as it should be or as readers would like to see it, but as it was. The following description of a tenement in New York City is an example of this kind of writing. Howells toured the tenements of lower Manhattan in 1896; by that time many of the Irish immigrants had moved out, and the new wave of immigrants from eastern Europe had moved in. In this article Howells describes the apartment of an Irish family living in one of the tenements. He contrasts the relatively happy Irish family to an unidentified one he had visited only minutes before, marveling at how comfortable the Irish Americans felt in their dirty, unventilated rooms.

We had our choice which door to knock at on the narrow landing, a yard wide at most, which opened into such tenements to the right and left, as many stories up as the stairs mounted. We stood at once in the presence of the hostess; there was no ceremony of sending in our cards here, or having our names called to her. In one case we found her over the washtub, with her three weeks' babe bundled in a chair beside it. A table, with a half-eaten loaf, that formed her

William Dean Howells, *Impressions and Experiences*. New York: Harper & Brothers, 1896.

breakfast, on it, helped, with the cooking-stove, to crowd the place past any possibility of sitting down, if there had been chairs to sit in; so we stood, as people do at an afternoon tea. At sight of us the woman began to cry and complain that her man had been drunk and idle for a month and did nothing for her; though in these times he might have been sober and idle and done as little. Some good soul was paying the rent for her, which was half as great as would have hired a decent flat in a good part of the town; but how her food came or the coal for her stove remained a mystery which we did not try to solve. She wiped her tears at the exhibition of a small coin, which she had perhaps dimly foreseen through them from the moment they began to flow. It was wrong, perhaps, to give her money, but it was not very wrong, perhaps, for the money was not very much, and if it pauperized her it could not have been said that she was wholly unpauperized before she took it. These are very difficult cases, but all life is a hopeless tangle, and the right is something that does not show itself at once, especially in economical affairs.

In another tenement we found a family as gay and hopeful as this was dismal and desperate. An Irish lady with a stylish fringe of red hair decorating her forehead, welcomed us with excuses for the state of the apartment, which in the next breath she proved herself very proud of, for she said that if people were not comfortable in their houses it was because they were slovenly and untidy. I could not see that she was neater than her neighbor on the landing below. She had a florid taste in pictures, and half a dozen large colored prints went far to hide the walls, which she said, the landlord had lately had whitewashed, though to eyes less fond than hers they showed a livid blue. The whitewashing was the sole repairs which had been put upon her tenement since she came into it, but she seemed to think it quite enough; and her man, who sat at leisure near the stove, in the three days' beard which seems inseparable from idle poverty, was quite boastful of its advantages. He said that he had lived in the court for thirty years and there was no such air anywhere else in this world. I could readily believe him, being there to smell it and coming away with the taste of it in my mouth. Like other necessaries of life, it must have been rather scanty in that happy home, especially at night, when the dark fell outside and a double dark thickened in the small bin which stood open to our gaze at the end of the room. The whitewash seemed not to have penetrated to this lair, where a frowzy mattress showed itself on a rickety bedstead. The beds in these sleeping-holes were never made up; they were rounded into a heap and seemed commonly of a coarse brown sacking. They had always a horrible fascination for me. I fancied them astir with a certain life which, if there had been a consensus of it to that effect, might have walked off with them.

All the tenements here were of this size and shape—a room with windows opening upon the court and at the rear the small black bin or pen for the bed. The room was perhaps twelve feet square and the bin was six, and for such a dwelling the tenant pays six dollars a month. If he fails to pay it he is evicted, and some thirty thousand evictions have taken place in the past year. But an eviction is by no means the dreadful hardship the reader would perhaps imagine it. To be sure, it means putting the tenant on the sidewalk with his poor household gear in any weather and at any hour; but if it is very cold or very wet weather, the evicted family is seldom suffered to pass the night there. The wretched neighbors gather about and take them in, and their life begins again on the old terms; or the charities come to their aid, and they are dispersed into the different refuges until the father or mother can find another hole for them to crawl into. Still, natural as it all is, I should think it must surprise an Irishman, who supposed he had left eviction behind him in his native land, to find it so rife in the country of his adoption.

Irish Workers in the Late Nineteenth and Early Twentieth Centuries

Kevin Kenny

In this selection from his book *The American Irish*, historian and Boston College professor Kevin Kenny explains the social progress of Irish Americans at the turn of the twentieth century. While the Irish immigrants who came to the United States in the middle of the nineteenth century were forced to take low-paying, unstable jobs, their children and grandchildren, along with later immigrants from Ireland, found that their job prospects improved as the years progressed. Kenny writes that as their numbers grew, Irish workers played a large role in the American labor movement, thus helping to improve working conditions for all Americans.

To understand the social position of the American Irish in the early twentieth century, it will be helpful to take a brief retrospective look at the late nineteenth century. In the 1880s and 1890s the number of American Irish confined to manual, unskilled jobs had begun to decline significantly. . . .

During the last two decades of the nineteenth century . . . both the first and the second generation of American Irish (the immigrants and their offspring) made significant

Kevin Kenny, *The American Irish: A History*. Harlow, UK: Pearson Education Limited, 2000. Copyright © 2000 by Pearson Education Limited. All rights reserved. Reproduced by permission.

social progress. By 1900, indeed, the Irish (both generations combined) had achieved rough occupational parity
with the native-born, and greatly surpassed the 'new immigrants' from southern and eastern Europe. As a pre-
dominantly urban people, the American Irish were concentrated much more heavily than the national average in
skilled and unskilled labour rather than in agriculture.
But, allowing for this urban-rural divide, their occupational structure closely resembled the national average:
while 65 per cent of American-Irish males worked in industry and transportation, only 15 per cent were unskilled
manual labourers, most of them recent immigrants. About
6 per cent belonged to the middle class and 14 per cent to
the lower middle class, while 15 per cent worked in agriculture. Only in New England, with its more rigidly stratified social structure and its long history of nativism, did
the American Irish remain heavily concentrated in menial
labour. But New England was home to fewer than one-fifth
of all Irish Americans in 1900.

Instead of being concentrated in menial labour, as they
had been for much of the nineteenth century, the American Irish now worked disproportionately in the skilled
trades. Most Irish-American workers were skilled rather
than unskilled, and they were disproportionately concentrated in the best-paid and most highly unionized trades.
While Irish Americans in 1900 accounted for only 7.5 per
cent (one-thirteenth) of the total male workforce in the
United States, they provided one-sixth of all teamsters,
metal workers and masons; one-fifth of stone cutters,
leather tanners, wire-workers, brass-workers, skilled textile workers, paper mill workers, roofers and street rail
workers; and almost one-third of all plumbers, steam fit-
ters and boiler-makers. In addition, they exceeded their
proportion in almost every other form of skilled and semi-
skilled urban employment, providing about 10 per cent of

all electricians, miners, glass-blowers and blacksmiths, and one-eighth of machinists, railroad-men, and printers.

Largely because of the arrival of the 'new' immigrants, the Irish were now less concentrated in manual labour than they had been; but many Irish-Americans, especially recent immigrants, continued to work in unskilled labour and rates of social mobility varied widely from region to region. In heavy industries like iron, steel and mining, Irish Americans now dominated blue-collar managerial posts, while the heaviest, lowest-paid labour was done by newly arrived Slavs, Hungarians and Italians. Even as late as 1900, however, 25 per cent of Irish-born males and 17 per cent of American-born Irish males still worked in unskilled, poorly paid and usually non-unionized jobs, and Irish Americans accounted for a disproportionately high per centage (11 per cent) of the nation's casual labourers. Irish economic progress was greatest in the Midwest and Far West, considerable in the dynamic economies of Pennsylvania and New York, and least in the relatively static and socially stratified states of New England.

As for Irish-American women, those who were native-born tended to avoid domestic service for work as secretaries, stenographers, nurses or schoolteachers. In the first decade of the twentieth century, daughters of Irish-born parents made up the largest group of schoolteachers in New York City, over 2,000 out of a total female teaching population of 7,000. Similar patterns were evident in cities throughout the Northeast, and in Chicago and San Francisco. In 1908, to take one example, American-born daughters of Irish parents made up 26.2 per cent of all teachers in Buffalo, 26.4 per cent in Fall River, 49.6 per cent in Worcester, 29.9 per cent in Lowell, 24 per cent in Providence, 38 per cent in Scranton and 15.5 per cent in New Orleans. Immigrant women, however, did less well than the native-born, with a substantial majority of Irish-born females still working either as servants or in textile factories and sweatshops in the early twentieth century. In 1900, 54 per cent of Irish-born women in the American labour force were house servants (compared to only 19 per cent of the second generation Irish), 6.5 per cent were laundresses and most of the remainder worked in industry. . . .

The Irish Americans and the Labour Movement

Hundreds of thousands of Irish immigrants [tried] to make a living in the United States in the early twentieth century. The American Irish by this time had come to dominate the trade union movement of the United States, shaking off most of their nineteenth-century reputation for violence and replacing it with an image of moderation and respectability. The American Irish played a dispro-portionately large role in the American labour movement at this time, providing more than eighty long-term labour leaders in over fifty prominent unions between 1890 and 1914. Even in trades where they accounted for only a small minority of the workforce, Irish Americans often domi-nated the union leadership, for example in the Carpenters and Joiners, Brewery Workers and Meat Cutters. 'Numer-ically,' as one historian puts it, 'the Irish dominated few trades, but politically they dominated a majority.'

While these unions were mainly concerned with 'bread and butter' issues of better wages and conditions, some Irish-American activists continued the tradition of radi-calism pioneered by Patrick Ford in the 1880s. That tradi-tion had been carried on in the following decade by men like Hugh O'Donnell, who led the striking steel workers of Homestead, Pennsylvania against the Pinkertons[1] in 1892, and by Sylvester Kelleher, who worked with the socialist

1. the Pinkerton Detective Agency, often hired by managers to break strikes

leader Eugene V. Debs on the American Railroad Union. The old association of Irish-American workers with violence did re-emerge in the early twentieth century when the MacNamara brothers of the Union of Bridge and Structural Iron Workers allegedly blew up eighty-seven buildings between 1905 and 1911, culminating in the notorious destruction of the offices of the *Los Angeles Times*, with twenty-one fatalities. Many Irish Americans were also involved in the radical anarcho-syndicalist organization, Industrial Workers of the World (IWW), which was founded in 1905 and was widely, if rather hysterically, accused of sustained violence and industrial sabotage throughout the following decade.

Perhaps the best-known Irish radicals involved in American labour circles in the early twentieth century were James Connolly and James Larkin. Born in Edinburgh, Scotland of Irish parents in 1868, Connolly moved to Dublin in 1896, where he founded the Irish Socialist Republican Party. He came to New York in 1902 where he published the *Harp*, established the Irish Socialist Federation and co-founded the Industrial Workers of the World (IWW), before returning to Ireland in 1910. The author of the classic *Labour in Irish History* (1910) and several other works, Connolly formulated a unique synthesis of socialism, republican nationalism and Catholicism, bringing his own Citizen Army to fight in the Dublin insurrection of 1916 in hopes of turning it into a social revolution as well as a nationalist one. A signatory of the Irish Declaration of Independence and a commander of the republican forces in the insurrection, he was executed by the British in the aftermath of the uprising. James 'Big Jim' Larkin (1876–1947) was even more prominent in American labour circles. Born in Liverpool of Irish parents, be organized a series of famous strikes in Belfast and Dublin between 1907 and 1913, before moving to the United States, where he was active in radical causes until his return to Ireland in 1923, devoting much of his energies to the IWW and to the American Communist party, which he helped found in the wake of the Bolshevik revolution of 1917.

While some Irish-American trade unionists, such as John J. Murphy of Central Labour Union in Philadelphia, also pursued a radical course, most Irish labour leaders in the early twentieth century were known for their conservatism. By 1900 Irish immigrants or their descendants held the presidencies of over 50 of the 110 unions in the American Federation of Labour (AFL), the most powerful but also one of the most conservative labour organizations in the country. The typical Irish-American labour activist was not an immigrant from the Irish countryside but a second- or third-generation American who had been raised in an industrial town or city. The AFL concentrated on winning better wages and conditions for its members, most of them highly skilled workers. These workers were mainly white, male and of northwest European descent; blacks, women and the 'new immigrants' from southern and eastern Europe were largely excluded from this narrow and restrictive labour movement. Concerned with 'bread and butter' issues, and confined to a skilled elite, the AFL deliberately avoided programs for systematic social reform, let alone revolutionary change.

Irish Americans headed some of the most influential unions within the AFL. Among the most prominent were James O'Connell of the Machinists; Timothy Healy, leader of the International Brotherhood of Stationary Firemen; Frank Duffy and P.J. McGuire of the Carpenters; and James Lynch of the Typographers. McGuire, an erstwhile socialist who had been instrumental in the creation of America's Labour Day, abandoned his earlier radicalism and cooperated with the leader of the AFL, Samuel Gompers, in creating a socially conservative, job-conscious union. Irish-American labour leaders also played an active role in assisting Gompers in his campaign against socialism within the AFL. John Mitchell, the leader of the powerful United Mine Workers of America, formed a special group, the Militia of Christ for Social Service, to coordinate anti-socialist policies in the labour movement and to gain the support of the Catholic Church. Irish-American unionists like John Hynes of the Sheet Metal Workers and Dan Tobin of the Teamsters also joined Gompers in withdrawing the AFL from the new International Federation of Trade Unions in 1919, on the grounds that involvement in international solidarity could only distract the AFL from its purpose of safeguarding its members' material interests.

By the early twentieth century, Irish-American women as well as men were playing a prominent role in the American labour movement. Leonora O'Reilly (1870–1926), the daughter of the Irish-born labour activist Winifred O'Reilly, was appointed to the board of the National Women's Trade Union League (WTUL) when it was founded in 1903. Mary Kenny O'Sullivan, who had been the first female organizer of the Knights of Labour in the 1880s, established the New York chapter of the WTUL. Agnes Nestor was elected president of the International Glove Workers Union, while Julia O'Connor was chosen to head the telephone operators' department of the International Brotherhood of Electrical Workers in 1912. Cork-born Mary Harris Jones (c.1830–1930), known as 'Mother Jones', was one of the foremost labour activists in the United States. Jailed frequently, she devoted most of her life to helping impoverished and exploited workers, and was particularly active among coal miners. In 1905 she helped found the IWW, where she was joined by Irish-American activist Elizabeth Gurley Flynn (1890–1964). The organization was headed by William 'Big Bill' Haywood (1869–1928), who was also of Irish descent.

The Butte Miners' Union

The labour struggles of the early twentieth century sometimes involved a generational conflict between established
Irish immigrants and the newest arrivals. This was certainly the case in Butte, Montana, the rather unlikely
venue for 'the most Irish town in the United States' at this
time. In 1900, the first and second generation Irish numbered over 8,000 in a total population of just over 30,000.
Thus, in this city fully 2,500 miles away from the nearest
eastern seaport, 26 per cent of the residents were either
Irish-born or the children of Irish-born. Butte was the
largest and most productive copper-mining town in the
world. It was settled from the beginning by Irish immigrants, a clear majority of whom came from the western
portion of County Cork, where copper was also mined.
Working in close cooperation with the legendary Irish-
born 'copper king', Marcus Daly, the first generation of
immigrants organized themselves in the socially conservative Butte Miners' Union, which emphasized job security,
company stock options, the prerogatives of skilled mine
workers over the unskilled and the exclusion of 'new immigrants'. The BMU never once launched a strike or work
stoppage in its thirty-six-year history.

From the turn of the century onward, however, the
BMU faced a mounting challenge from radicals in the IWW
and the Western Federation of Miners (WFM). The WFM
was led by Donegal-born Ed Boyce, who moved its headquarters from Butte to Denver to escape the BMU. There
followed a wave of strikes and labour violence in Butte, in
which recent Irish immigrants played a prominent part.
The immigrants now came from all over Ireland, supplant-
ing the dominance of the Corkmen who had long constituted a powerful regional enclave within the Irish-American community in Butte. Whereas the older immigrants
had been concentrated in mining, the newer ones favoured

heavy industry. Differences in cultural background and work experience translated into radically different understandings of labour and social justice. In the words of one historian, 'By 1910 some Irish immigrant workers had been in Butte for thirty years; others for thirty days. To assume that they shared either ethnic or class interests is folly. They arose from and occupied different and mutually hostile worlds.' Shunning existing ethnic institutions like the Ancient Order of Hibernians and the Robert Emmet Literary Association, these 'new' Irish founded their own Pearse-Connolly Independence Club (named after the two most influential leaders of the 1916 rebellion in Ireland), sharing meeting space with the IWW and other radical groups. They were supported in their efforts by Irish socialist Con Lehanc, who visited Butte in 1916, and by Jim Larkin, who visited three times between 1915 and 1917. The causes of Irish liberation and social justice in America were inextricably linked, Larkin insisted, echoing James Connolly and Patrick Ford.

Illegal Irish Immigrants

John Doherty

Many of the Irish immigrants who came to the United States in the nineteenth century found their way to Boston. They settled in Irish neighborhoods and eventually gained a stronghold in the city, particularly in the area of politics, and they have continued the tradition of protecting their own into the twenty-first century. In this article John Doherty examines how illegal immigrants from Ireland—those who remain in the United States without the proper documentation—have been protected not only by Boston's large Irish population but also by the U.S. Immigration and Naturalization Service, which until recently has focused primarily on nonwhite non-English-speaking illegal immigrants. However, after the bombing of the World Trade Center in 1993, Congress passed stiff laws against those who stayed in the United States beyond the length of time permitted on their visas. Irish American senator Ted Kennedy from Massachusetts, along with others in Congress, had hoped to have those laws relaxed, and the vote in the House to do so was scheduled for September 11, 2001. However, after the terrorist attacks that occurred that day, few politicians wanted to roll back immigration standards, and today not even the highly protective Irish leaders in Boston can prevent the Immigration and Naturalization Service from deporting Irish immigrants who have remained in the United States illegally.

A fistfight erupted inside Scruffy Murphy's in Dorchester [Massachusetts] right before Christmas. Witnesses say the drunken brawl was over a girl, and that it began when one young man head-butted another. It landed one of the men in the back of a police cruiser and the other with a summons—not exactly an unfamiliar scene late at night along Dorchester Avenue. But this fight was different. It sent a chill through the neighborhood, and out to Brighton, Somerville, and Allston, where many of Boston's Irish live.

Irish and undocumented, the two young men became the stuff of urban legend. This would be no drunk-and-disorderly beef or drawn-out string of trivial court appearances. By the next night, word had spread down the street from Scruffy's to Nash's and then all over the capital of the illegal Irish nation that agents from the Immigration and Naturalization Service (INS) had arrived at police headquarters after the arrest, and that the boys, both part of Boston's vast, clandestine Irish exile world, were ferried off. Whether to jail or to the Auld Sod [Ireland], no one knew.

"No one's going home for Christmas this year," one young Irish man—who has lived undocumented in Boston for seven years—said at the time. "Not this year. If you leave now, you're never coming back."

Protecting Their Own

They were bulletproof, Boston's Irish. An Irish-man with an out-of-date passport, expired visa, or, for that matter, no visa at all, had little cause to fear being deported from this town. Take, for example, what happened when Congress passed tough new immigration laws in the mid 1990s in reaction to the Oklahoma City bombing and the first World Trade Center explosion: Forty Guatemalans living illegally in Boston were sent packing by the local office of the INS. So were 243 Dominicans and 16 Cape Verdeans, among others. Of the city's illegal Irish community—which some estimates put at 5,000 of the 25,000 Irish nationals who help make Boston the undisputed seat of Irish

America—the number deported totaled four.

"All these deportations and no Irish," says Victor Do-Couto of the Massachusetts Immigrant and Refugee Advocacy Coalition. He pauses. "Gee, I wonder why that is?"

Sarcasm like DoCouto's is a measure of how much of an open secret was the underground network of illegal Irish in this town, protected by the economic and political clout of the established Boston Irish. A whole covert support system was headquartered in the dark, smoke-filled interiors of Irish pubs in Dorchester and Allston where undocumented Irish could get jobs with Irish contractors and other employers who weren't too particular about work visas, cash their paychecks, hook up with sympathetic landlords, and find cheap cars for sale.

"Getting swallowed up into the community never really presented a problem," says Padraig O'Malley, an Irish-born senior fellow at the John W. McCormack Institute of Public Affairs at UMass Boston. As for politicians, he says, "it's a matter of looking after your constituents, and when the biggest block of constituents are Irish or belong to Irish organizations, then you cater to their needs. That's been true for more than 100 years, all the way back to Tammany Hall.[1] Of course, it's unfair, but it's also true that ultimately we're all part of a tribal system."

Crackdown on Illegal Immigrants

But now, suddenly, Irish immigrants are standing alongside Dominicans and Cape Verdeans in the crosshairs of the immigration bureaucracy. This crackdown seems to be sticking, threatening a subculture that has been part of the Boston landscape for decades, and it's putting everyone who is not a bona fide American on notice: Have your papers in order. The "or else" is understood. "The truth is,

1. the scene of political corruption in nineteenth-century New York City

Irish have been among those being picked up [by the INS] since September 11 [2001]," says Kieran O'Sullivan of the Irish Immigration Center in Boston. "They've been stopped at the airport, everything."

One Irish pub owner jokes about the good old days, when a routine underage drinking check or a scuffle that drew the cops may have raised a few heartbeats, but that's all. "Half my bar staff, half my clientele," he says, "nobody has documents." Police never asked about anyone's immigration status. "The cops used to cut you some slack, but now they have no choice. They have to see your documents, have to call INS."

That's why bar owners frown on allowing video recorders these days—out of deference to the undocumented. No cameras, either. And any after-hours crap that could attract attention, like the incident on Dorchester Avenue, is dealt with harshly.

"The word is out," says Connell Gallagher, publisher of the area's *Irish Emigrant* weekly newspaper. "You just can't screw around like you used to."

And if you're Irish in Boston, that's saying something.

The 2000 census may have concluded that Asians, blacks, and Hispanics now make up the majority of Boston's population, but those were just statistics. Boston is an Irish town. The Irish dominate, in business, in politics, in sheer numbers. Twenty-five percent of state residents, asked by the census to describe their ethnic identity, called themselves Irish, the highest concentration in the country, outnumbering the second most populous group—Italians—by more than two to one. With just 2 percent of the total U.S. population, Massachusetts is home to 4 percent of all Irish Americans. It's no mystery why the American Ireland Fund has its international headquarters here—or how it managed to collect an impressive $2.2 million at its annual black-tie affair in November

[2001], which was attended by the city's elite, at the same time other charities were struggling to compete for money with the post–September 11 relief efforts.

The Irish in Boston

For years, of course, the Irish have been a special case in Boston's swirling immigrant mix. Irish history is among the most celebrated in a city obsessed with its own role in America's past. For the Irish of Boston, the story is a proud tale of beating back the discrimination of the Brahmin establishment. Beginning in the mid 1800s, the Irish were blamed for a rise in crime and depicted as welfare cases and drunkards. Their allegiance to their new country was questioned because of their suspicious loyalty to a Roman pope. They came anyway, to escape famine, civil war, and an industrial economy that had left them behind. They took dangerous jobs for low pay and lived in crowded tenement houses. And they got a foot in the door. Today, reproductions of the "no Irish need apply" signs that once hung in Boston shop windows can be found framed and mounted proudly as a sort of badge of honor in the well-appointed suburban homes of third-, fourth-, and fifth-generation Irish. And whether they stay in Southie and Dorchester or move to Milton or Dedham, the Irish remain unfailingly reliable voters. "They came and they began to vote," says Thomas O'Connor, a Boston College historian and author of *The Boston Irish*. "And they continue to vote."

The Irish cemented their long and impressive rise to political power in Boston with the election of Hugh O'Brien as mayor in 1884, and broadened their influence with the ascendancy of U.S. House Speaker Thomas P. "Tip" O'Neill, the Kennedys, and others. How influential were they? By the time Congress ran a lottery to hand out 40,000 new visas to applicants from 34 countries in 1991, two Massachusetts politicians—Senator Edward M. Kennedy and then-Congressman Brian Donnelly—led the efforts to set almost half of them aside exclusively for immigrants from just one place: Ireland.

And, in fact, the Irish kept on coming, the vaunted Irish economic miracle notwithstanding. While the flow has fallen from the peak of 20,000 Irish per year who left their home country for the United States in the 1980s, an estimated 6,000 to 8,000 Irish made the trip annually during the 1990s, many to Boston, according to the Irish Episcopal Commission for Emigrants.

"There may still be building jobs in Dublin," says Kevin O'Neill, head of the Irish Studies Program at BC [Boston College]. "But for a young guy in rural Ireland, it's sometimes easier to pick up stakes and move to Boston. The networks are in place here."

Tough New Immigration Laws

For leaders of other ethnic immigrant communities, those networks have always been a source of envy, if not frustration—and the attention the INS now seems to be paying to the undocumented Irish was a long time coming.

For these other groups, American immigration law had become increasingly restrictive. Tough new rules that Congress passed in 1996 made it easier for foreigners to be deported. Deportation could even be imposed for past crimes. Portuguese families in New Bedford and Fall River reported relatives being packed up and sent back to the mid-Atlantic islands of the Azores for misdemeanors committed years or even decades earlier. Activists in Boston and Brockton began a campaign against what they saw as a process of singling out the burgeoning Cape Verdean population.

The INS moved detainees at will. A Dominican arrested on immigration charges in Boston could find himself housed in a cell rented in Hillsborough, New Hampshire, then shipped to Oklahoma, away from relatives and lawyers. Longtime permanent residents of Massachusetts disappeared into a black hole. Portuguese officials estimate that as many as 400 American Portuguese, most of them from Massachusetts, were deported to the Azores; many had been living in America since the 1970s.

The Irish never felt the same bite of those laws. The reasons, experts say, were obvious. White and English-speaking, the Irish don't attract the same attention as dark-skinned foreigners. "You're virtually invisible," says Do-Couto of the Immigrant and Refugee Advocacy Coalition. "You can speak the language. You don't have physical characteristics that set you apart like Central Americans or Brazilians do." More than that, the city's heavily Irish police, court, and political machines kept the newcomers out of harm's way or, at the very least, smoothed the way when any ran afoul of the law. Sympathetic local prosecutors could be urged to reopen cases and lower sentences for relatively minor crimes to just under one year—the cutoff at which the INS comes knocking. It may not be politically correct, immigration lawyers say, but an educated, middle-class Irish kid, who can express regret for his transgressions, makes a better case for such a so-called "revise-and-revoke" than a poor Creole- or Spanish-speaking member of an immigrant community beset with the poverty and crime that helped land him in court in the first place.

The advantage the Irish have is social and economic—not political—says Brian O'Neill, a Boston immigration lawyer and nephew of the legendary House speaker. "If the charge is leveled that the Irish are somehow getting away with murder here, I think the argument could be made that Irish assimilation into our culture is easier. The Irish bring with them not just white skin and English as a first language, but a familiarity with the legal system in their country that doesn't differ radically from our own.

The justice system in some [other] countries, often inefficient and corrupt, doesn't correspond in the same way."

On one front, at least, the Irish did have a problem: overstaying visas. Many had grown accustomed to overstaying temporary work or student visas because they knew they could simply straighten things out later. This changed in 1996. Overstaying a visa for more than 180 days now means an automatic ban of three years on returning to the United States. An Irishman who went back to Dublin on the frequent cheap flights out of Logan could find himself turned away when trying to reenter.

Kennedy and other lawmakers, including Congressman Barney Frank, pushed hard to have those laws relaxed. And they were making headway. A package of bills, many of them written by the Massachusetts delegation, passed the Senate [in the summer of 2001]. It was aimed at rolling back the tough new immigration standards to the pre-1996 rules.

A vote in the House was scheduled for September 11 [2001].

After the terrorist attacks that day, no one in Congress wanted to soften anything associated with immigration. To no one's surprise, Kennedy's proposed reforms fell by the wayside. A subsequent attempt to tack the changes onto the Border Security Bill failed. September 11 had managed to do what the booming Celtic Tiger economy back home and the tough changes to deportation law in 1996 could not: stem the flow of illegal Irish immigrants into Boston.

"I've seen a huge difference in levels of enforcement," says Eoin Reilly, a Boston immigration attorney who sheds his tie and provides pro bono legal advice in Irish pubs and elsewhere. "A lot more people are being turned back. There really is a lot more anxiety in the community, and it's because there's a lot more scrutiny."

CHAPTER 4

Portraits of Irish Americans

John L. Sullivan

William D. Griffin

Boxer John L. Sullivan was one of the first true Irish American sports legends. He rose to fame in the late nineteenth century, just as Irish Americans were beginning to make significant progress socially and economically. In this profile of Sullivan, William D. Griffin describes how Sullivan began his athletic career and how he transformed boxing with his clean fighting style. Griffin is a professor of history at St. John's University in New York.

In his heyday . . . John Lawrence Sullivan was more than a celebrity, he was a national hero, adored by millions, in a way that no prizefighter—and certainly no Irish American—had ever been esteemed before. Yet he was no better a man—and, in some ways, a worse one—than his predecessors. As a realistic commentator put it: "He was a drunkard, this god. He was a loudmouthed, vulgar, oversized bully. At least for the greater part of his life he was a spoiled, irresponsible, disagreeable roughneck. An S.O.B. [son of a bitch] of the first water . . . if he ever drank any. Yet he was a god."

Sullivan's status reflected not only the new acceptability of pugilism as a legitimate sport, but the acceptability of the Irish as Americans. For all his popularity in the immigrant community, John L. was very definitely an American. He was, in fact, typical of the blustering self-confident, vulgar "go-getter" that was taking over American

William D. Griffin, "The Great John L.," *The Book of Irish Americans*. New York: Times Books, 1990. Copyright © 1990 by William D. Griffin. All rights reserved. Reproduced by permission of Times Books, a division of Random House, Inc.

society in the late nineteenth century. Although he did make a pious pilgrimage to his father's birthplace, he was less than impressed by the typical village welcome to the returning Yank. On being shown the ancestral homestead, he blurted out: "I guess the old man was a good judge, to get out of here."

How Sullivan Got His Start

Born in 1858, the "Boston Strong Boy" evaded his mother's genteel aspirations to steer him into the priesthood, and became a plumber's apprentice—a job he lost when he broke his boss's jaw in a dispute. He began earning money with his fists when he was nineteen, and soon came under the shrewd management of William Muldoon. A succession of victories over increasingly more prestigious fighters led, at last, to his famous confrontation with the reigning heavyweight champion, Paddy Ryan.

The match, on February 7, 1882, was the last championship contested under the old London Prize Ring rules—bare knuckles, the ring pitched on bare turf, the rounds marked by knockdowns. Despite the remote location of the match, in Mississippi City, Mississippi, Sullivan's growing reputation and Muldoon's adroit public relations had attracted a big crowd and national attention. After a comparatively short nine rounds, Sullivan landed the blow that gave the United States a new champion.

Although Sullivan did fight later bare-knuckle matches (notably the epic seventy-five-round battle with [American boxer] Jake Kilrain in New Orleans in 1889 [for the Heavyweight Championship of America]), he much preferred the new rules of boxing that had been developed in England by the marquis of Queensberry. These involved padded gloves, rounds of fixed duration, a hard-floored ring, and no wrestling, gouging, or spitting, such as the old London rules (which survived in America long after they

John L. Sullivan, seen here in an 1889 match with Jake Kilrain, transformed boxing with his clean fighting style.

had been dropped in London) permitted. Sullivan advocated a quick, clean contest of strength and his advocacy helped win acceptance for the marquis's[1] rules in the United States. Thus Sullivan did much to transform the prize ring "from an animalistic slaughter house into an arena of pugilistic skill."

Sullivan traveled to the British Isles and Australia to maintain his status as not merely America's but the world's greatest boxer. A typical "brag" went as follows: "I challenge any and all of the bluffers who had been trying to make capital at my expense to fight me either the last week of August this year, or the first week in September at the Olympic Club, New Orleans, for the purse of twenty-five thousand dollars and an outside bet of ten thousand dollars, the winner of the fight to take the entire purse. First come, first served. I can beat any man in the world. . . ."

1. John Sholto Douglas, or the marquis of Queensberry, was a boxing promoter who developed a set of boxing rules in 1867.

Sullivan's Reputation

Sullivan's sayings ("The bigger they are, the harder they fall") and pronouncements were on everybody's lips. Music hall performers endlessly repeated the line: "Let me shake the hand of a man that shook the hand of John L. Sullivan!" It was reported that Sullivan called on the president whenever he was in Washington, even though his opinions and actions seemed to arouse more interest than those of the White House's occupants. A reporter portrayed the great man at the peak of his fame:

And then John L. Sullivan, raw, red-faced, big fisted, broad shouldered, drunken with gaudy waistcoat and tie, and rings and pins, set with enormous diamonds and rubies—what an impression he made! Surrounded by local sports and politicians of the most rubicund and degraded character (he was a great favourite of them), he seemed to me, sitting in his suite at the Lindell, to be the apotheosis of the humorously gross and vigorous material. Cigar boxes, champagne buckets, decanters, beer bottles, overcoats, collars and shirts littered the floor, and lolling back in the midst of it all in ease and splendour, his very great self, a sort of prizefighting J.P. Morgan.

"Aw, Haw! haw! haw!" I can hear him even now when I asked him my favourite questions about life, his plans, and the value of exercise etc. "He wants to know about exercise! You're all right, young fella, kinda slim, but you'll do. Sit down and have some champagne. Have a cigar. Give him some cigars, George. These young newspaper men are all right to me. I'm for 'em. Exercise? What I think? Haw! haw! Write any damn thing yuh please, young fella, and say that John L. Sullivan said so. That's good enough for me. If they don't believe it, bring it back here and I'll sign it for yuh. But I know it'll be all right and I won't stop to read it neither. That suit yuh? Well, all right. Now have some more champagne and don't say I didn't treat yuh all right, 'cause

I did. I'm ex-champion of the world, defeated by that little dude from California, but I'm still John L. Sullivan—ain't that right? Haw! haw! They can't take that away from me, can they? Haw! haw! Have some more champagne, boy."

After ten years as champion of the world, an overweight and overconfident John L. Sullivan went down to defeat on September 7, 1892. Outboxed and outmaneuvered for twenty-one rounds by the younger, lighter James Corbett, the exhausted Sullivan finally collapsed under a flurry of blows to the head. An unprepared and stunned sporting world had lost its most picturesque and popular figure.

Sullivan never fought again. Taking his downfall (after 200 victories) in good spirits, he became an actor (an occupation almost as congenial to his temperament as fighting) and, after finally giving up liquor, a temperance lecturer. When he died in 1918, despite the rigors of a Boston winter and the distractions of a world war, thousands of loyal admirers gathered to pay their last respects.

Corbett, the son of a San Francisco stable hand, was also an "Irishman," but he never captured the fancy either of his fellow Celts or of the public at large as Sullivan had. Newspapermen, impressed by his sophisticated air and his stylish clothes, dubbed him "Gentleman Jim" (he had, in fact, been a bank clerk); the Boston Irish dismissed him as a "Western dude." John L. had been a link to the harsh but glorious days of [early nineteenth-century Irish boxer] Dan Donnelly, a link between Ireland and America. After his time, boxing would never be quite the same.

Joseph P. Kennedy

David Burner

Joseph P. Kennedy was the great-grandson of Irish immigrants who fled Ireland during the famine. He was also the father of the first Irish Catholic president of the United States, John F. Kennedy, and senators Robert Kennedy and Ted Kennedy. In this article David Burner describes how Kennedy became one of the wealthiest men in Massachusetts, his marriage to Rose Fitzgerald, and how he groomed his children to enter the world of politics. Burner is a history professor at the State University of New York at Stony Brook.

The widowed mother of the American-born Patrick ("P.J.") Kennedy squeezed out a living running a notions shop. The young Patrick dropped out of school and worked for some time as a stevedore. Later, after having become proprietor of a neighborhood saloon that he had financed from his own and his mother's savings, he chose politics as a second career. His tactics of dispensing advice and friendship to those in need and of giving free beer to voters enabled him to enter the Massachusetts state senate. Soon he was importing Haig & Haig Scotch, selling it to Boston's better hotels and restaurants. In 1888 he seconded Grover Cleveland's nomination for the presidency of the United States. Nicknamed the "Mayor of East Boston" and known as one of the city's four most influential politicians behind the scenes, Patrick Kennedy later earned his living both as a liquor wholesaler and as a

David Burner, "Being a Kennedy," *John F. Kennedy and a New Generation*, edited by Oscar Handlin. Boston: Little, Brown and Company, 1988. Copyright © 1988 by David Burner. All rights reserved. Reproduced by permission of Little, Brown and Company, Inc.

banker. His marriage to Mary Hickey, the sister of the mayor of Brockton, benefited his social and economic status. Although Patrick and Mary played classical music and a daughter has described her father as idealistic and her mother as visionary, they still maintained an insular, provincial life on the islands in the harbor that made up East Boston. Boston's politics were now, for better or worse and doubtless for both, largely dominated by the Irish, and one of P.J.'s descendants would eventually rise on that base to leadership of his country. It was not, however, a politics controlled by a single machine like a Tammany Hall.[1] Individual clan chieftains such as Martin Lomasney, Daniel Coakley, James Michael Curley, and John Francis Fitzgerald used ruthless tactics to keep their supporters in line, and John F. Kennedy's father and grandfather laid claim to an area in Massachusetts comprising parts of Cambridge, Brighton, and Waltham that ultimately provided JFK with a congressional seat.

Joseph Patrick Kennedy's Youth

P.J.'s son, Joseph Patrick Kennedy (1888–1969), began his progress out of the Irish ghetto into the wider worlds of business, politics, and diplomacy when his parents transferred him from East Boston's Xaverian school to the famous Boston Latin School. This was a clear if unintentional exodus from a community indrawn and carefully guarded by such injunctions as Archbishop William O'Connell's frequent warning to the faithful not to send their children to Protestant schools. Both as a boy and as a man the young Joe Kennedy steadily pursued wealth. "How can we make some money?" was a characteristic childhood greeting. Like [the first Irish American presidential candidate] Al Smith, he hawked newspapers on the

1. the headquarters of the New York political machine

urban sidewalks, becoming streetwise and meeting pimps, prostitutes, and racketeers. As captain of his parochial school's baseball team, the Assumptions, Joe used his earnings to buy eye-catching baseball uniforms and took on a genteel team, the Playfairs, whom his boys thrashed. In college Joe earned some $10,000 by operating a sightseeing bus line through the older section of Boston.

At Boston Latin the good-looking gregarious Joe prepared for Harvard. An unattentive student, Joe took an extra year to earn his diploma, playing baseball and football, managing the basketball team, commanding a drill regiment, and getting elected class president. The school yearbook predicted that he would make his mark "in a very roundabout way." Harvard accepted him as until the 1950s it did practically any scion of a successful family. At Harvard Joe switched from the difficult study of economics to the less demanding field of music. He kept his love for classical music nearly hidden: it might appear not quite "muscular" enough for a practical businessman and politician. He rarely read a book, either in college or in later life. Though successful in athletics and in making friends, Joe was denied membership in the best Harvard social clubs. Some thought this exclusion to be because he was an Irish Catholic, but one Harvard faculty member recalls a different story: Joe was blackballed for his habitual lying.

Upon graduating, Joe chose banking as a quick route to attain his goal of becoming a millionaire by his mid-thirties. At first he rejected politics because he believed it would inevitably lead to defeat, as well as a dependency on a fickle public rather than on his own inner strength. As he later said to his wife, he wanted "the freedom which money provides, the freedom to come and go where he pleased, when he pleased and how he pleased." To learn the trade, he worked briefly at his father's East Boston Columbia Trust Company. Soon he became assistant bank examiner for the state. "If you're going to get money," Kennedy explained, "you have to find out where it is." Within two years he borrowed to save Columbia Trust from a merger and to assume the presidency of the small bank. He claimed to be but was probably not the nation's youngest bank president. Joe Kennedy's political knowledge matured as he observed the effect of legislation on banks.

The Fitzgeralds

High ambition and zest for life led Joseph Kennedy to the doorstep of Rose Fitzgerald, daughter of Boston's colorful Mayor John Fitzgerald. Known as "Fitzie," and later as "Fitz" or the syrupy "Honey Fitz," his ancestry also reached back to County Wexford. That family, too, had Americanized itself. Rose's grandfather, John Francis Fitzgerald, the son of a peddler turned successful grocer, was born in 1863 in the North End of Boston, an immigrant district where three infants out of ten died before reaching the age of one. But John's parents prospered, and in 1879 they removed their newsboy son from the streets to Boston Latin School. Upon graduating he entered Harvard Medical School but left without a diploma when his father died. This act must have been a result of custom rather than need, for his father had left a considerable estate. John then apprenticed himself to a local boss whom he followed with absolute fidelity. In 1889 he married Mary Hannon, a quiet girl with a sunny disposition.

The Fitzgeralds' daughter Rose, born in 1890, was brought up as a member of the Irish upper classes. Placing third academically in her high school and being voted the prettiest senior, she entered the Convent of the Sacred Heart on Commonwealth Avenue in Boston. It had been her wish to attend Wellesley College, but Archbishop O'Connell persuaded her father not to send her to a secular college. "My greatest regret," she recalled, "is not having gone to Wellesley College. It is something I have felt a little sad about all my life." The next year her father, fearing political scandal after his first term as mayor, sent her to a Catholic finishing school at Blumenthal in Northern Germany. There she became accomplished in German and French and absorbed a curriculum of *Kinder, Kirche, Küche*—children, church, and cooking. The school was cold, and its discipline rigid. Every Sunday morning all the students gathered in the chapel for an evaluation of each girl's conduct, which included such faults as walking too fast or failing to curtsy before a religious statue. Rose may have lost a little of her spontaneity and independence at the German school, but after returning home, she ran charitable and social clubs at Manhattanville College (another branch of the Convent of the Sacred Heart), studied piano in Boston at the New England Conservatory of Music, participated in a little theater group, and became the youngest member of the Boston Public Library's book selection committee. She described herself as "the leader of the young Catholic set in Boston."

Honey Fitz enjoyed a long colorful career. He would sing "Sweet Adeline" at the slightest provocation. Once when a runaway truck ran him down after he had moved some children from its path, he would not let an ambulance take him to the hospital until he sat up and sang his trademark song to reassure onlookers he was all right. When Franklin D. Roosevelt later sent him on a goodwill tour, Honey Fitz sang "Dulce Adelina" from Colombia to Argentina. "He could talk to you," according to an acquaintance's recollection, "for ten or fifteen minutes at the rate of 200 words a minute, without letting you get in more than two or three times, then pat you on the back and tell you how much he enjoyed the conversation." Like other ethnic politicians of his day, Honey Fitz was able to make city politics accessible to ordinary people in a way that Brahmin bluebloods often could not. He had a "wake squad" who, on his behalf, attended every wake in the city. His victorious campaign for a second nonconsecutive mayoral term charged his opponent with anti-Catholicism. Fitz has left a reputation for taking graft and overloading the city payroll with incompetent cronies while at the same time building schools and hospitals in the slums; later he was removed from Congress on charges of voting fraud.

Burgeoning Businessman

Fitz allowed that Joe Kennedy's Harvard background and bank presidency made him an acceptable suitor. Joe and Rose were married in 1914, settling into a house in Protestant, middle-class Brookline, Massachusetts. Joe's banking experience equipped him to be treasurer of Old Colony Realty, which offered middle-class suburban sites to the new Irish, where they would be safe from "the encroachment of undesirable elements." It also bought up defaulted mortgages and evicted poor Irish and Italian families before repainting and reselling their homes. During World War I Joe served as assistant general manager of Bethlehem Steel's shipyards at Quincy, earning $20,000 a year. Joe knew nothing of shipbuilding but all about financing; he eventually developed an ulcer while breaking production records, building thirty-six destroyers in two years. When Kennedy refused to send two frigates to Argentina without first getting paid for them, four United States Navy tugs with armed servicemen towed the boats away on the orders of Assistant Secretary of the Navy Frankin D. Roosevelt. The two men thereby learned mutual respect. Joe told his friend William Randolph Hearst that Roosevelt was even tougher than Joe was himself.

As the turn of the century was the age of the banker in the United States, the mid-1920s would be the start of the great bull market. In the twenties Joe learned almost all there was to know about manipulating the stock market, profiting heavily from insider trading. He believed that corporations existed for the benefit of the management, not the stockholders. But money, disappointing the American trust in it, does not quickly buy a place in patrician society. In the years when Kennedy was growing up, Boston newspapers carried one society section for the Irish and another for the Americans of older lineage. The Kennedys were not fully accepted socially either in the Protestant summer resort of Cohasset or later in Hyannis Port on Cape Cod, where the family sported a chauffeur-driven, plum-colored Rolls Royce. Kennedy was refused summer membership in the Cohasset Golf Club, and the Cape's season list of debutantes did not carry the names of his daughters. In 1926, while keeping his summer home on the Cape, Joe finally moved his rapidly growing family by private railroad car to Westchester County in New York—first, temporarily, to Riverdale and then to the restrictive community of Bronxville. The Kennedys were caught between classes; while they preferred not to associate with the lower-class Irish, many Yankees still snubbed them. A few years later Kennedy objected to a newspaper's calling him an Irish-American. Puzzled, he said, "I was born here. My children were born here. What the hell do I have to do to be an American?"

Leaving behind these class distinctions as well as his wife (after the last child was conceived in 1931 Rose declined for religious reasons to have sexual relations with him), Joe Kennedy went to Hollywood in the late 1920s. For some three years he participated in an industry that was bursting with sudden and freewheeling money-making as it catered to a demand of its own creation. Every week 60 million Americans went to the movies. Kennedy made some $6 million on cheaply made Tom Mix [actor who played a cowboy] westerns and melodramas like *A Poor*

Girl's Romance and *Red Hot Hooves.* He temporarily abandoned these potboilers upon beginning an affair with Gloria Swanson, the reigning queen of Hollywood silent films. "Gloria needs handling," said a tipster who informed him of her waywardness with money. Swanson, already married three times, was twenty-eight, a good age for a film star to be in those days when cameras and lighting required very young actresses. Joe placed her in the infamous *Queen Kelly,* directed by the daring perfectionist Erich von Stroheim. Kennedy ultimately withheld the film, which portrays a self-giving prostitute nun, from distribution, ostensibly for moral reasons. In the 1950 movie *Sunset Boulevard,* in which Swanson brilliantly played an aging movie actress and von Stroheim played her butler and confidant, a sequence from *Queen Kelly* is shown. Joe managed to hand the actress much of the financial loss for *Queen Kelly* and to offset his own loss through winnings on Swanson's first talking picture, *The Trespasser.* Their romance ended when, according to the actress, she questioned his opinion on a small matter, and Joe chose to return to New York. Recognizing the shakiness of the economy, he sold his common stock holdings just before the stock market crash of 1929.

Raising the Family

By the end of the 1920s Joe and Rose Kennedy had eight children. Raising young Kennedys was a joint project. Rose superintended them with both vigor and painstaking care, keeping files on them, strategically planting reminder notes or abbreviated paper lectures, placing clocks in every room so the children would not be late for dinner or Mass. The father, when home, ruled the children firmly. Rose schooled the children in such points as the correct use of "I" and "me" so that they could speak properly in Joe's presence, and before dinner they were required to read news stories tacked on a bulletin board in preparation for discussion with him. Sometimes the family conversation concerned the fundamental national issues of the day. At other times one of the children assumed the role of a Founding Father and argued points based on *The Federalist Papers*.[2] While many of the "conversations" consisted of Joe's lectures or questions eliciting factual responses from his sons, the overall effect created in young Jack Kennedy a craving to read and a capacity to memorize masses of information. In general, the boys attended Protestant preparatory schools, whereas the girls were sent to Catholic schools.

The Kennedy family compound at Hyannis Port was especially fit for the training of male offspring. It was a place for calisthenics at dawn; Wheaties for breakfast; lectures from the father; and practice in the patrician sport of sailing, perfected by the elder Kennedy as he followed the boys in a separate boat, barking out their mistakes over a bullhorn. The sport was patrician; but the concentration was on winning, not on the graceful and courteous excellence of the *aristoi* [aristocracy]. "Don't play unless you can be captain," Joe Kennedy is supposed to have proclaimed, along with "Second place is failure." A son who performed badly was sometimes forced to eat in the kitchen, and Joe Kennedy, Jr., once won a race with an oversized sail. Is it that the father, so eager for entrance into the upper classes, was forever simply missing the point, which is that the well-mannered sportsman plays for the sake of good manners? Or was he quite consciously seeking triumphal vindication on his own terms in place of acceptance on theirs, confident that after a correct interval of haughty rejection, older society will yield to new money and power?

Joe Kennedy courted the socially established Anglo-

2. Written by American statesmen Alexander Hamilton, James Madison, and John Jay, these papers supported the ratification of the U.S. Constitution.

American classes by using tactics that violated the codes to which those classes claimed to subscribe. Those tactics brought wealth to Joe, which he used to buy for his children an education in more polite ways of living. His aggressiveness would become a component in the characters of his offspring. In Jack Kennedy that aggressiveness was combined with an element of fastidious withdrawal which suggests that in him the education took hold.

The local Catholic culture must also have presented mixed messages. The religion of the Nazarene poor has found many formulas for justifying wealth, but at a sacrifice to simple consistency. The local ethnic Catholicism also reconciled piety with hard-bitten ambition and the rough ways of city politics. It further mingled economic progressivism with ideological conservatism. Many layers of social and moral history were compressed in the consciousness of three generations of Kennedys.

Joe's fatherly attention was returned with love and obedience. What children would not admire a father who could introduce them to the cowboy movie star Tom Mix or the sports heros [baseball great] Babe Ruth or [football great] Red Grange, and who instantly responded to their letters when away from home? Despite Joe's many trips away, the children correctly sensed that they were always on his mind. Some successful fathers can transmit only their wealth to their children; Joe Kennedy also passed on his unyielding determination. The exception was Rosemary, retarded and, after an operation, cared for at a convent. Joe showed his love for her by making heavy contributions to research on retardation.

Kennedy Becomes Involved in Politics

Joe Kennedy made another fortune in the stock market by selling short during its plunge from May 1930 to March 1933. Meanwhile, he was interesting himself in politics, particularly in an aspiring presidential candidate, whose steel he had tested during World War I. In 1930 he visited Franklin D. Roosevelt, then governor of New York. The Great Depression had frightened Kennedy, as it had many other American capitalists in the 1930s. Hungry people, he said, could turn "ugly and menacing," and something should be done for them. Roosevelt, of course, did not yet have the credentials that his New Deal would later give him. But Joe Kennedy shrewdly saw in him at least a possibility for national economic initiatives. He raised $150,000 for FDR and traveled with him on several campaign tours; he would always claim to have persuaded [wealthy newspaper magnate] William Randolph Hearst to break the convention deadlock that had held FDR back from an early win. The additional $50,000 that he lent the Roosevelt campaign was never repaid, but in company with FDR's son James, Joe went to Europe on a successful postelection trip to import "medicinal" liquor—Ron Rico rum, Haig & Haig Scotch, and Gordon's gin—just in time for the repeal of prohibition.

The important early backer earned a larger reward, somewhat grudging and belated because of opposition from Roosevelt's adviser Louis Howe. A Columbus, Ohio, campaign speech that Kennedy had written for Roosevelt carried a blueprint for the future Securities and Exchange Commission. In 1934 Roosevelt appointed the stock market insider as chairman of the commission, saying, as one practical man might say of another man equally unburdened with scruples, "It takes a thief to catch a thief." Perhaps Joe Kennedy's most effective innovation was to prohibit short sales at a price lower than the last to appear on the stock market ticker. He preferred conscientious self-regulation to new laws but enforced rules strictly against flagrant abusers. Corporate underwriting quadrupled under his management, and Kennedy received considerable praise for his work.

Joe Kennedy left the post in 1935 to write a campaign book. *I'm for Roosevelt*, published the following year, which argued that businessmen should be grateful to FDR for saving capitalism. Actually his journalist friend Arthur Krock did the writing; Kennedy had offered him $5,000 for the job. "It was useful," Joe observed elsewhere, "to have a Roosevelt who had the confidence of the masses," and could mollify them short of more radical programs. But the book embraced government planning uncritically, crediting Roosevelt with every economic gain since 1933. The volume contained at least one line of nonsense: "I have," Joe wrote, "no political ambitions for myself or for my children."

Ambassador Kennedy

Joe returned to government for a year as head of the Maritime Commission, with the object of invigorating the sickly shipbuilding industry. The great moment followed: his selection in 1938 as ambassador to Great Britain. With this appointment Kennedy had captured a high citadel of the Anglo-American aristocracy. Not yet believing that events in Europe deserved his concentrated attention, Roosevelt had evidently thought it a "grand joke" to tweak the lion's mane by appointing an unreconstructed Irishman to the Court of Saint James. When he first heard the suggestion, FDR "laughed so hard he almost fell out of his wheelchair."

The hot-tempered, gum-chewing ambassador delivered Roosevelt a pile of trouble. He called the queen of England a "cute trick" (he later revised that to a "dowdy housewife") and [English prime minister Winston] Churchill a "heavy drinker," but those references paled beside his apparent remark to the German ambassador. "I'm for Hitler." Family, not country, motivated Joe. In one speech at Aberdeen, he wrote: "I should like to ask you all if you know of any dispute or controversy existing in the world which is worth the life of your son, or of anyone else's son?" He also feared that communism would emerge from the rubble of a war. His appointment was proving disastrous for the United States. He praised the Munich settlement,[3] saying he could not imagine going to war for Czechoslovakia. In 1938 after Munich he told the Navy League: "The democracies and dictators should cooperate for the common good." FDR, unprepared for amicable remarks about the Fascists, informed Kennedy that he did not want his ambassador to continue arguing against American intervention in the European war that began in September 1939. Kennedy returned home in 1940. Because of an indiscreet interview, in which Joe told reporters that "democracy is finished in England," he exhausted his credit with Roosevelt and learned a painful lesson about discretion in politics. That episode put an end to his public career, but not the use of his influence on behalf of his sons, who were now to take up his march upon the fortresses of the Brahmin class.

3. Under the September 1938 settlement, Germany was given the Sudetenland and control over Czechoslovakia in exchange for agreeing not to further attack Europe. Adolf Hitler soon reneged on that promise.

Frank McCourt

Interview by the Academy of Achievement

Frank McCourt was born in Brooklyn, New York, in 1932 to Irish parents. When McCourt was four his family decided to move back to Ireland, and he did not return to the United States until 1949. Not long after his return he joined the army. McCourt later attended college and became a teacher and writer. His first book, *Angela's Ashes*, was published in 1996 and won the Pulitzer Prize for Biography. The book tells the story of McCourt's childhood in Limerick, Ireland. In 1999 McCourt published the sequel *'Tis*. In this interview by the Academy of Achievement, McCourt describes his experiences as an Irish immigrant in America. He tells of his loneliness and how he was conscious of his accent and his lack of education. Eventually McCourt discovered that he had many stories to tell about his years in Ireland, a discovery he cites as a turning point.

[*Academy of Achievement:*] *What were you thinking when you came to America at the age of 19. Out of this background, full of anger at your circumstances, at the church, at the lack of opportunity, what was in your mind when you came here? What were you looking for?*

[*Frank McCourt:*] When I arrived here my condition was very poor, emotionally, psychologically, even physically. I had no self-esteem because of what I came from. No education. Everybody was saying, "Oh, you have to have a high school diploma in this country." I couldn't say I only went to primary school in Limerick.

Academy of Achievement, "Frank McCourt Interview," www.achievement.org, June 19, 1999. Copyright © 1999 by the Academy of Achievement. Reproduced by permission.

The minute I opened my mouth they'd say, "What you should do is join the cops." I didn't want to join the cops. So I didn't know what to do with myself since I had no self-esteem. I was very angry over having no education. I didn't know what to do with myself. I didn't know how to find the door into America. Here I was. I didn't know anybody. So I was mostly alone and floundering.

Other people come from Italy and Czechoslovakia and places like that, and they have to grapple with America, and they have to grapple with trying to master the English language as well. At least I had the language: that made it more convenient for me. But I had to deal with something else that people rarely talk about. It's an ethnic story in a way.

The minute I opened my mouth then they'd say, "Oh, you're Irish." Suddenly I'm labeled. I wasn't a human being, in Ireland I was just a low-class type, but here I'm a low-class Irish type, an Irish low-class type. So I didn't know. Somehow I had to deal with that. "Oh, you're Irish." And at that time, that was 1949, there was still some kind of a lingering residue of prejudice against the Irish. People used to tell me, all the people, up and down New England (I'm in New York) there would be signs saying, "No Irish need apply."

I was a bit simple as if I had just come off a farm. And I knew better than that. I knew I was better than that. People who—Irish-Americans who were running elevators and working as porters, they were looking down on me, and I knew then that I was again at the bottom of the heap.

I was confused most of the time. I never had anything but the dream of getting out of this.

I wanted to be something else but I didn't know what. There was no clear cut dream. I thought I'd like to have a job, a decent job in an office. I'd like to be in an office sitting behind a desk, pushing papers around, making little decisions about pushing papers, get out at 5:00 o'clock, meet this gorgeous girl and we'd probably get married and have two-and-a-half kids and live out in Long Island or someplace like that, and I'd go to mass every Sunday morning, be nice and warm and clean, and I'd be accepted, and I'd lose my Irish accent, and I'd sound like James Cagney. I didn't know what to do. I read a lot.

That's what I did. I read and read and read voraciously and widely. Then I was liberated from this menial job I had in a hotel. I was the man with the dust pan and the broom in the lobby. I was liberated by the Chinese who attacked Korea and America drafted me and sent me to Germany for two years. I don't know what I would have done if the Chinese hadn't attacked Korea. I'm a victim of history in Ireland and I'm a beneficiary of history in America.

McCourt Becomes a Writer

When did you first know what you wanted to do with your life?

Well, I always wanted to write but I didn't know how to go about it. I didn't have the courage of certain people that you hear about. I read something about [American writer] Shelby Foote recently who wrote a story for the *Saturday Evening Post* when he was 19 and that was it. He was on his way. Or other people like Scott Fitzgerald. He had a college education and so on, but I didn't know where to begin and I didn't know what to write. I certainly was not going to write about my experiences growing up in this slum in Ireland. Then something happened when I finally went to NYU.

We were asked to write about a single thing, an object in our childhood. And the object that meant most to me that was so significant was the bed I slept in with my brothers, all four of us. This half acre of a bed with a disaster of a mattress, which collapsed in the middle. Everybody peed in the bed, so the spring was gone, and we tried to keep it together with bits of string, but after a while the acid from our bodies rotted the string. We'd get into bed and we'd roll into the middle, the four of us, and fight. "Get out of my way."

And if you had to go to the john you went to a bucket and so on and came back. And we were—we'd light a candle to get at the—and we'd hold the candle and we'd go slapping at each other's legs and bodies killing the fleas. That was probably the most concrete image I brought away from my childhood and I wrote about that. The professor gave me an "A+." And I said, "Jesus, this is very strange." And then he says, "Please read this to the class." And I said, "No." "Would you?" "No." "Would you please?" I said, "No, I'd be ashamed." And he read it. He said, "Do you mind if I read it?" So he read it to the class and I think they sensed that I was the one who wrote it, and good looking girls started looking at me in an interested way, but I thought they'd be—I thought they'd be disgusted. But I found myself being stalked leaving the class that day. "Is that how you grew up?" And it seemed—I seemed to suddenly have become kind of an exotic in the class.

That stuck in my head. I still wasn't convinced that this was the material of my writing but I kept going with notebooks, and making lists of people I grew up with, the streets in Limerick, the shops, the priests and everything else. That was a turning point.

The encouragement of that one teacher?

That one teacher. The one in Ireland, Mr. O'Halloran, who told me I was a literary genius and this man at NYU. One little thing can change the course of your life, or can change your emotional landscape.

Gabriel Byrne

Interview by Brad Balfour

Actor, producer, director, and writer Gabriel Byrne was
born in Dublin, Ireland, in 1950. Byrne, who now lives in
New York City and Dublin, has starred in many feature
films, including *Excalibur, Miller's Crossing*, and *The
Usual Suspects*, as well as several television programs and
miniseries. In this interview by editor and journalist Brad
Balfour, Byrne discusses his early years as an actor and explains what it means to him to be Irish in America. Americans, he contends, make certain assumptions about Irish
people, such as that they are melancholy and poetic. He
also says that at first being Irish in America was a problem
for him because there were few people from outside the
United States in American film.

*Brad [Balfour]: You haven't done theatre in a long time.
It's great because you get to have a more of a normal life
since you have kids and seem to be a person who has
enough of a real life to know how it works.*

Gabriel [Byrne]: My kids live in New York and I moved
back to NY to be with them. As a convenience I began to
consider theatre as a reality. I had done a lot of films but
for some years had entertained in my head the fantasy of
going back to the stage, because that's where I really began. I started at the Project Theatre in Dublin which was
basically a converted warehouse in Essex St. in the middle
of Temple Bar before it became fashionable. It was then a
ghost town, just warehouses and buildings boarded up. In

Brad Balfour, "The Brooding Dubliner . . . and Proper New Yorker Gabriel Byrne,"
Irish Connections, vol. 1, June/July 2000. Copyright © 2000 by *Irish Connections*. Reproduced by permission.

the middle of this wasteland, which is the center of Dublin ironically enough, was the Project Theatre. We were right beside a tiny little shop run by two women who had been there since 1920 and all they sold was bread and milk. Liam Neeson, Neil Jordan, Stephen Rea, Jim Sheridan, Colm Meany, we all began in that small little theatre. There wasn't any alternative at the time because theatre was the only way to gain experience as an actor. The Gate and the Abbey were institutions that none of us could ever aspire to because you had to train to get into the Abbey and you had to have a classical drama education to get into the Gate so that didn't fit any of our CV's [curricula vitae]. We really were part of that first artistic explosion of Dublin in the late '70s and early '80s. U2 were just happening at that time, film was beginning to happen in a very small way. It was a very exciting time, my memories of theatre are very exciting. But obviously once I moved to London I found films very addictive; I loved film and always have. But the stage is really where actors are tested. There's a testing of an actor that just doesn't happen in a movie. When you walk out on stage you have to bring the audience to you and you only have you and the words to do it. Whereas in film a bad performance can be made to look good on screen and good performance can be made to look mediocre. You are really at the mercy of the director and this team, including the editor, cinematographer, and so forth. But that's not why I came back to the theatre. I just felt it was time to redefine myself again as an actor.

It's a chance to reassess yourself as a person.

It has been hugely important to me this play [*Moon for the Misbegotten* by Eugene O'Neill]: physically, emotionally, artistically, spiritually. There are letters here from people who have come to see the play and have been moved and touched by it in a way that I could never comprehend. It's changed me in very many ways. I'm so glad that I had the courage to do it because there was a time that I sincerely wanted to run in the opposite direction and not do it.

You mean theatre itself?

No, this particular play. Coming back was a big deal, you had to make yourself so vulnerable and you had to expose yourself to the possible humiliation.

You're playing a failed actor, an alcoholic. It's a classic Irish thing. You have all these burdens on you. It's fascinating how you pull it off creatively and visually. It's a very measured, understated role, compared to how Roy [Doctrice, a British actor] can be so broad and Cherry [Jones, an American actress] so dramatic.

Yes the dramatic arc of this character is a very subtle one. In that the ultimate emotional climax that you have to hit every night can't be by necessity quick, it has to unfold gradually. I'm playing an actor, but what's interesting about playing anything is that what you are really playing is a person. What that person actually does for a living is really incidental, you play the person. I felt an enormous sympathy and a tenderness for this man who is based on a real person. He really did live a lot of a things he says in the play, that climactic last emotional scene really did happen. So in a way, you have a responsibility to embody as well as you can this man's crippled life, death and Eugene O'Neill's benediction of him. So in a couple of strokes I establish him as an actor, once the audience is told he's an actor, the audience will believe he's an actor. Actors, weirdly enough, are like everyone else in that they have the same emotions, needs and desires. More or less, as human beings, we share the same vocabulary. Yes, it is a different style of playing to the way Roy and Cherry play. I don't know if that's a result of my work in film or my instinctive need for understatement. As an actor I'm very much a minimalist, I don't like to do too much, I like to suggest and let the audience fill in as much as possible. Any part you are playing, you are trying to capture the spirit of someone, and this wounded man who is desperate for forgiveness is someone we can all identify with. O'Neill is an amazing playwright and perhaps the most honest of all the American playwrights because he rips open the body and pulls out the guts, saying 'this is what we are.' He doesn't dress it up in any fancy idealization to be a human being. But at the same time all his characters are shot through with a mirror to who we are as human beings first and foremost. If he was just specifically an Irish playwright, or an American playwright he would have a limited kind of appeal. I've always thought of him as universal playwright in the same way Shakespeare is. O'Neill is not a Catholic or Irish or American. He is a universal commentator on the human condition. There is a connection between alcoholism and the Irish but I have to point out that it's a very common assumption that the Irish and alcohol go together. The reality is that on the table of correlation between alcoholism and nations per capita head, we are seventh down the line. The stigma is no longer true.

Overcoming Misconceptions About Being Irish

People have a misunderstanding here. It's being re-examined.

Yes, I hope so. There are certain assumptions made about Irish people, like that ridiculous quotation by [English writer] GK Chesterton where he said the Irish were a race that god made mad for all their wars were merry and all their songs were sad. I mean that's a ridiculous quote, but I've seen it used seriously by people as a definition of what the Irish character is. The Irish are prone to melancholy, they are poetic, they foam at the mouth with literary epilepsy, they are great storytellers, the greatest talkers since the Greeks, they are war-like, they are always fighting about religion, they are drunks. . . . There are more labels attached to being Irish. Now there's a new one that's crept in that they are cool and hip.

See what you guys did, you, Jim Sheridan. . . .

When I came to America I had a real problem, and still do to a certain extent, with being Irish in America. There are very few European actors who work in Hollywood in the top leagues because European actors are regarded as outsiders. And once you have an accent you are regarded as being different. If you look at American films, not only are there very few Irish or English people in them but you rarely see a Korean just playing a Korean, or a Hispanic just playing a Hispanic. They are always labeled or type-cast in this culture of labels. The immigrant view is excluded from a great deal of mass culture. When I look at the audience in this theatre, I don't see a Hispanic or Chinese and I only very rarely see anyone from the black community. Theatre here appeals to a white, upper class—moneyed audience who can afford to go. Mainstream American culture in movies is basically formulaic and is also geared towards the predominance of one cultural view. Although it's a multiracial society, it's not reflected in the form that we associate theatre with. One rap song is more relevant to the vast majority of young people [than] theatre is or movies are. Being Irish is to have a label around your neck which [is] misleading. I know a hundred different Irish people in NYC who have a hundred different personalities.

You've played within the Irish and European frameworks and at the same time do all kinds of American work—independent and commercial, like The Usual Suspects. *What allows you to make those transitions?*

I've always chosen projects I feel say something about something. I've never actually chosen a bad script, but the amount of scripts that turn in great movies are in the minority. That goes for every actor, you look at Robert Mitchum's biography, there's maybe ten great movies there and there are a hundred that aren't memorable. I've always tried to do films that have a little bit of risk in them and I've always tried to stay out of the mainstream where there is a huge trap. Ironically one of the worst things that can happen as an actor is to have a huge hit. When you are associated with that hit they don't want you to be anything else. What I've tried to do is jump from genre to genre. I believe this business is about longevity and variety. I don't want to be a guy playing the same role over and over. I'm not trying to have another hit that makes more money than the one before. I've always refused to be pigeon-holed so I'll turn up in something that's totally unexpected. One of the things that Liam [Neeson] has talked about is the importance of retaining your Irishness, and at the same time if they want to play an Israeli or a Frenchman, you can do it.

CHRONOLOGY

1678
The first known Irish immigrants come to the American colonies as indentured servants.

1737
The first recorded St. Patrick's Day parade takes place in Boston, Massachusetts.

1790
The first U.S. government census shows that forty-four thousand Irish immigrants live in the United States.

1810
The Irish newspaper *Shamrock* begins publication in New York City.

1817
Construction on the Erie Canal begins, and many Irish immigrants begin to come to the United States to get jobs digging the canal.

1828
Andrew Jackson, son of Irish Protestant immigrants, becomes president of the United States.

1830
Beginning in this decade, Irish immigrants come to help lay the many railroad tracks being placed across the United States.

1836
Maria Monk's *Awful Disclosures* is published, confirming the fears of many Americans about the Catholic Church.

1838

British Parliament passes the Poor Law, which taxes land-lords not only for the amount of land they own but also for the people who live on the land; the law results in landlords beginning to evict tenants from their land.

1839

The Irish Emigrant Society is formed in New York City to help new immigrants.

1840

About 1 million people of Irish descent live in the United States.

1844

Reacting to the growing number of Irish immigrants, an anti-Catholic mob riots in Philadelphia.

1845

A potato famine caused by the fungus *Phytopthora infestans* hits Ireland; many immigrate to the United States.

1846

The Irish people become severely affected by the famine; St. Patrick's Battalion, made up primarily of Irish Americans, is formed by deserters from the U.S. Army and fights with the Mexican army; Tammany Hall listens to the many Irish immigrants in New York City and nominates Irish American Mike Walsh as state assemblyman; he is elected and later becomes a congressman.

1847

The Poor Law Extension Act provides for more work-houses to be built so the newly homeless will have a place to live.

1848

San Francisco hires its first Irish police chief.

1850

The fungus that caused the famine disappears from Ireland; the Irish Emigrant Society establishes the Emigrant Savings Bank.

1851

By this date more than 300,000 Irish people live in workhouses; 216,000 Irish immigrants, more than ever before, come to the United States.

1854

The Know-Nothing Party, formed in part as a reaction to the influx of immigrants to America, captures every statewide office in Massachusetts.

1855

The city of New York opens Castle Garden, its first immigrant processing center; by this time, 27 percent of the members of the New York City Police Department are Irish.

1858

The Fenian Brotherhood, a group of Irish Americans working for Irish independence, forms in New York City.

1861

The Civil War begins in the United States; by the end of the war, more than 144,000 Irish will have fought on either side.

1863

The draft riots take place in New York City in July as mostly Irish mobs protest against the Conscription Act; more than one hundred people are killed.

1866

The Irish American organization the Fenian Brotherhood devises a plot to invade Canada, but they are forced to retreat in June.

1870
New York City is now home to two hundred thousand people born in Ireland.

1880
New York City elects its first Irish Catholic mayor, William R. Grace; by this time there are more than 6 million Catholics in the United States.

1916
In Ireland the people rebel against British oppression on Easter; the rebellion is now called the Easter Uprising; the event strengthens the feelings of many Irish Americans for Irish independence.

1928
Alfred E. Smith becomes the first Irish American to be nominated for president of the United States; he loses to Herbert Hoover.

1960
John F. Kennedy, who has Irish roots, is elected president of the United States.

1981–1990
During this decade about thirty-two thousand Irish immigrants come to the United States.

1991–2000
In the 1990s nearly fifty-seven thousand people emigrate from Ireland to the United States.

2002
The number of people who emigrated from Ireland to the United States is 1,419.

Early Irish Immigrants

Terry Coleman, *Going to America*. Garden City, NY: Anchor, 1973.

Thomas Gallagher, *Paddy's Lament: Ireland 1846–1847, Prelude to Hatred*. New York: Harcourt Brace Jovanovich, 1982.

Edward Laxton, *The Famine Ships: The Irish Exodus to America*. New York: Henry Holt, 1996.

James J. Mangan, ed., *Robert Whyte's 1847 Famine Ship Diary: The Journey of an Irish Coffin Ship*. Dublin: Mercier Press, 1994.

Kerby Miller, *Emigrants and Exiles: Ireland and the Irish Exodus to North America*. New York: Oxford University Press, 1985.

Kerby Miller and Paul Wagner, *Out of Ireland: The Story of Irish Emigration to America*. Washington, DC: Elliott & Clark, 1994.

Janet Nolan, *Ourselves Alone: Women's Emigration from Ireland, 1885–1920*. Lexington: University Press of Kentucky, 1989.

Arnold Schrier, *Ireland and the American Emigration, 1850–1900*. Chester Springs, PA: Dufour Editions, 1997.

The Great Famine

Robert Dudley Edwards, *Great Famine: Studies in Irish History, 1845–1852*. New York: New York University Press, 1957.

Christine Kinealy, *This Great Calamity: The Irish Famine, 1845–1852*. Boulder, CO: Roberts Rinehart, 1995.

John Percival, *The Great Famine: Ireland's Potato Famine, 1845–1851*. New York: Viewer Books, 1995.

Irish American History

Tyler Anbinder, *Five Points: The Nineteenth-Century New York City Neighborhood That Invented Tap Dance, Stole Elections, and Became the World's Most Notorious Slum*. New York: Free Press, 2001.

Michael Coffey, ed., *The Irish in America*. New York: Hyperion, 1997.

William D. Griffin, *The Book of Irish Americans*. New York: Times Books, 1990.

Karen Price Hossell, *Immigrants in America: The Irish Americans*. San Diego: Lucent Books, 2003.

Kevin Kenny, *The American Irish: A History*. New York: Pearson Education, 2000.

Charles R. Morris, *American Catholic: The Saints and Sinners Who Built America's Most Powerful Church*. New York: Times Books, 1997.

George W. Potter, *To the Golden Door: The Story of the Irish in Ireland and America*. Boston: Little, Brown, 1960.

William V. Shannon, *The American Irish*. New York: Macmillan, 1963.

Ronald Takaki, *A Different Mirror: A History of Multicultural America*. New York: Little, Brown, 1993.

Carl Wittke, *The Irish in America*. New York: Russell & Russell, 1956.

Later Irish Immigrants

David Burner, *John F. Kennedy and a New Generation.* Boston: Little, Brown, 1988.

Maureen Dezell, *Irish America: Coming into Clover: The Evolution of a People and a Culture.* New York: Doubleday, 2000.

Ray O'Hanlon, *The New Irish Americans.* Boulder, CO: Roberts Rinehart, 1998.

Web Sites

Interpreting the Irish Famine, 1846–1850, www.people. virginia.edu/~eas5e/Irish/Famine.html. This Web site provides extensive information on the Irish potato famine. Contents include photographs, narratives, and newspaper and magazine articles written during the famine.

Views of the Famine, http://vassun.vassar.edu/~sttaylor/ FAMINE/index.html. Articles and illustrations contemporary to the famine are available on this Web site.

INDEX

Academy of Achievement, 185
Act of Union (1800), 36–37
Adams, Henry, 145
Adams, William Forbes, 63
African Americans
  anti-Irish sentiment among,
    104–105
  compared to Irish, 101–102
  Irish antagonism toward,
    102–103
American Communist Party,
  154
American Irish, The (Kenny),
  149
American Irish Fund, 161
*American Protestant
  Vindicator* (newspaper), 90
Ancient Order of Hibernians,
  16, 157
Angela's Ashes (McCourt), 185
anti-Catholicism
  Americans' views of Irish and,
    25
  in nineteenth-century U.S.,
    85–96
  violence and, 91–93
Atlantic Monthly (magazine),
  96
Awful Disclosures (Monk),
  88–89, 90

Balfour, Brad, 189
Ball, Judy, 36
Bannon, John, 128
Beecher, Lyman, 86

Beirne, Joseph A., 20
blacks. *See* African Americans
boarding houses, 25–26
Border Security Bill, 165
Boston, 158–60
Boston Pilot (newspaper), 104
Britain
  hatred for, among Irish
    immigrants, 83–84
  response of, to potato famine,
    39, 40–43
  view of Irish in, 40
  view of Irish migration in, 27
Brooklyn Eagle (newspaper),
  118
Bruce, John E., 105
Burner, David, 172
Burr, David, 23
Butte Miners' Union, 156–57
Byrne, Gabriel, 189–94

Callahan, Nelson J., 23
Canada, as destination of
  emigrant ships, 53
Capston, James L., 128
Catholics Telegraph
  (newspaper), 126
Chesterton, G.K., 192
Chinese, compete against Irish
  laborers, 99–101
Civil War, Irish in, 115–29
  in Confederate army, 120
  support for Union among, 102
  in Union army, 115–16
Clark, Hugh, 92

202